POWER
FROM ON HIGH

A SELECTION OF ARTICLES ON
THE SPIRIT-FILLED LIFE

BY

CHARLES G. FINNEY

CHRISTIAN LITERATURE CRUSADE
Fort Washington, Pennsylvania 19034

CHRISTIAN LITERATURE CRUSADE

U.S.A.
P.O. Box 1449, Fort Washington, PA 19034

BRITAIN
51 The Dean, Alresford, Hants SO24 9BJ

AUSTRALIA
P.O. Box 91, Pennant Hills, N.S.W. 2120

NEW ZEALAND
P.O. Box 1203, Palmerston North

ISBN 0-87508-190-8

This Printing 1994

PRINTED IN THE UNITED STATES

CONTENTS

Preface

Charles Finney lives on! Recently in Oregon I talked with a minister from Rochester, New York. In glowing terms he told me how that city recently celebrated the 150th anniversary of the great revivals under Finney. All churches joined the observance because those awakenings saturated and changed all classes of society, especially the higher classes. This tells us that in a great revival there is total coverage. The horizontal and human needs are met in a new way because the vertical working of God's Spirit in the churches is so strong.

Rochester actually experienced three revivals under Finney. Let us highlight the first one of 1830. Rochester was then a young city, full of new enterprises and full of sin. Finney says the revival swept through the town and changed the great mass of the most influential people, both men and women. This included many physicians and merchants. A large number of leading New York state lawyers lived there, and many were converted. The revival remolded public sentiment, and public affairs came into the hands of Christians with the controlling influence of the community on the side of Christ. Powerful conversions resulted in new leaders who became salt and light for society.

A strange part of the whole story is that Rochester at the time was considered to be "burnt-over revival territory." Finney at first had turned down the invitation to come to Rochester, favoring rather invitations to the larger cities as New York or Philadelphia. And when he did arrive in Rochester he found religion in a very low state. The churches were suffering from divisions.

It was in the first Rochester revival that Finney introduced the "anxious seat," inviting people to come forward to certain front seats "to a public renunciation of their sinful ways and a public committal of themselves to God." God gave immediate success to this step, and even the most influential heeded the call.

What brought on all this change? Back of it all was a prevailing spirit of prayer—not only prayer, but a strong and deep *spirit* of prayer, which continued to characterize the whole revival and carry it forward.

At a stop on the way to Rochester by canal boat a minister came aboard to converse briefly with Finney. Instead of getting off again he decided to go along to Rochester. As this man walked the streets there he began to weep and pray with a heavy burden: "Lord, I do not know how it is, but I seem to know that You are going to do a great work in this city."

Finney says, "The spirit of prayer was poured out powerfully, . . . so that some persons stayed away from the public services to pray, being unable to restrain their feelings under preaching."

The spirit of prayer in the churches was the secret. In that day, as in ours, many were in much darkness with regard to this greater praying. Finney says, "There must be in the church a deeper sense of the need of the spirit of prayer."

It is not that our congregations are prayerless. But so seldom do we find a church *with the spirit of prayer resting on the congregation.* That is what is missing; that is what must come back. That is the revival we need.

— *Mr. Armin R. Gesswein*
Reprinted from *Alliance Weekly,* February 1, 1984. Used with permission.

1

Power From on High

Please permit me through your columns to correct a misapprehension by some of the members of the late Council at Oberlin arising from the brief remarks which I made to them; first on Saturday morning, and afterwards on the Lord's Day. In my first remarks to them I called attention to the mission of the Church to disciple all nations, as recorded by Matthew and Luke, and stated that this commission was given by Christ to the whole Church, and hat every member of the Church is under obligation to make it his lifework to convert the world. I then raised two inquiries: (1) What do we need to secure success in this great work? (2) How can we get it?

Answer: 1. We need the enduement of power

1

from on high. Christ had previously informed the disciples that without Him they could do nothing. When He gave them the commission to convert the world, He added, "But tarry ye in Jerusalem till ye be endued with power from on high. Ye shall be baptized with the Holy Ghost not many days hence. Lo, I send upon you the promise of My Father." This baptism of the Holy Ghost, this thing promised by the Father, this enduement of power from on high, Christ has expressly informed us is the indispensable condition of performing the work which He set before us.

2. How shall we get it? Christ expressly promised it to the whole Church, and to every individual whose duty it is to labor for the conversion of the world. He admonished the first disciples not to undertake the work until they had received this enduement of power from on high. Both the promise and the admonition apply equally to all Christians of every age and nation. No one has, at any time, any right to expect success unless he first secures this enduement of power from on high. The example of the first disciples teaches us how to secure this enduement. They first *consecrated themselves* to this work, and continued in prayer and supplication until the Holy Ghost fell upon them on the Day of Pentecost, and they received the promised enduement of power from on high. This, then, is the way to get it.

The Council desired me to say more upon this subject. Consequently, on the Lord's Day, I took for my text the assertion of Christ that the Father is more willing to give the Holy Spirit to them that ask Him than we are to give good gifts to our children.

1. I said, This text informs us that it is infinitely easy to obtain the Holy Spirit, or this enduement of power from the Father.

2. That this is made a constant subject of prayer. Everybody prays for this, recurringly, and yet, with all this intercession, how few, comparatively, are really endued with this spiritual power from on high! This need is not met. The lack of power is a subject of constant complaint. Christ says, "Everyone that asketh receiveth," but there certainly is a "great gulf" between the asking and receiving that is a great stumbling block to many. How, then, is this discrepancy to be explained? I then proceeded to show why this enduement is not received. I said: (1) We are not *willing*, upon the whole, to have what we desire and ask. (2) God has expressly informed us that if we regard iniquity in our hearts He will not hear us. But the petitioner is often *self-indulgent*. This is iniquity, and God will not hear him. (3) The petitioner is uncharitable.(4) Censorious. (5) Self-dependent. (6) Resists conviction of sin. (7) Refuses to confess to all parties concerned. (8) Refuses to make restitution to injured parties. (9) He is prejudiced and uncandid. (10) He is resentful. (11) Has a revengeful spirit. (12) Has a worldly ambition. (13) He has committed himself on some point, and become dishonest

because he neglects and rejects further light. (14) He is denominationally selfish. (15) Selfish for his own congregation. (16) He resists the teachings of the Holy Spirit. (17) He grieves the Holy Spirit by dissension. (18) He quenches the Spirit by persistence in justifying wrong. (19) He grieves Him by a lack of watchfulness. (20) He resists Him by yielding to an evil temper. (21) Also by various dishonesties in business. (22) Also by indolence and impatience in waiting upon the Lord. (23) By many forms of selfishness. (24) By negligence in business, in study, in prayer. (25) By undertaking too much business, too much study, and too little prayer. (26) By a lack of entire consecration. (27) Last and greatest, by *unbelief.* He prays for this enduement without expecting to receive it. "He that believeth not God hath made Him a liar." This, then, is the greatest sin of all. What an insult, what a blasphemy, to accuse God of lying!

I was obliged to conclude that these and other forms of indulged sin explained why so little is received, while so much is asked. I said I had not time to present the other side. Some of the brethren afterward inquired, "What is the other side?" The other side presents the certainty that we shall receive the promised enduement of power from on high, and be successful in winning souls, if we ask, and fulfill the plainly revealed conditions of prevailing prayer. Observe, what I said upon the Lord's Day was upon the same subject, and in addition to what I had previously said. The misapprehension alluded to was this: If we first get rid of all these forms of sin, which prevent our receiving this enduement, have we not already obtained the blessing? What more do we need?

Answer. There is a great difference between the *peace* and the *power* of the Holy Spirit in the soul. The disciples were *Christians* before the Day of Pentecost, and, as such, had a measure of the Holy Spirit. They must have had the peace of sins forgiven and of a justified state, but yet they had not the enduement of power necessary for the accomplishment of the work assigned them. They had the *peace* which Christ had *given* them, but not the *power* which He had *promised.* This may be true of all Christians, and right here is, I think, the great mistake of the Church and of the ministry. They rest in conversion, and do not seek until they obtain this enduement of power from on high. Hence so many professors have no power with either God or man. They prevail with neither. They cling to a hope in Christ, and even enter the ministry, overlooking the admonition to wait until they are endued with power from on high. But let anyone bring all the tithes and offerings into God's treasury, let him lay all upon the altar and put God to the proof therewith, and he shall find that God "will open the windows of heaven, and pour him out a blessing that there shall not be room enough to receive it."

2

What Is It?

The apostles and brethren, on the Day of Pentecost, received it. What did they receive? What power did they exercise after that event?

They received a powerful baptism of the Holy Ghost, a vast increase of divine illumination. This baptism imparted a great diversity of gifts that were used for the accomplishment of their work. It manifestly included the following things: The power of a holy life. The power of a self-sacrificing life. (The manifestation of these must have had great influence with those to whom they proclaimed the gospel.) The power of a cross-bearing life. The power of great meekness, which this baptism enabled them everywhere to exhibit. The power of a loving enthusiasm in proclaiming the gospel. The power of teaching. The power of a loving and living faith. The gift of tongues. An increase of power to work miracles. The gift of inspiration, or the revelation of many truths before unrecognized by them. The power of moral courage to proclaim the gospel and do the bidding of Christ, whatever it cost them.

In their circumstances all these enduements were essential to their success; but neither separately nor all together did they constitute that power from on high which Christ promised, and which they manifestly received. That which they manifestly received as the supreme, crowning, and all-important means of success was the power to prevail with both God and man, the power to fasten *saving impressions* upon the minds of men. This last was doubtless the thing which they understood Christ to promise. He had commissioned the Church to convert the world to Him. All that I have named above were only means, which could never secure the end unless they were vitalized and made effectual by the power of God. The apostles, doubtless, understood this; and, laying themselves and their all upon the altar, they besieged the Throne of Grace in the spirit of entire consecration to their work.

They did, in fact, receive the gifts before mentioned; but supremely and principally this power to savingly impress men. It was manifested right on the spot. They began to address the multitude; and, wonderful to tell, three thousand were converted the same hour. But, observe, there was no new power manifested by them upon this occasion, except the gift of tongues. They wrought no miracle at that time, and they used these tongues simply as the means of making themselves understood. Let it be noted that they had not had time to exhibit any other gifts of the Spirit which have been above named. They had not at that time the advantage of exhibiting a holy life, or any of the powerful graces and gifts of the Spirit. What was said on the occasion, as recorded in the Acts of the Apostles, could not have made the impression that it did had it not been uttered by them with a new power to make a saving impression upon the people. This power was not the power of inspiration, for they only declared certain facts of their own knowledge. It was not the power of human learning and culture, for they had but little. It was not the power of human eloquence, for there appears to have been but little of it. It was God speaking in and through them. It was a power from on high — God in them making a saving impression upon those to whom they spoke. This power to savingly impress abode with and upon them. It was, doubtless, the great and main thing promised by Christ, and received by the apostles and primitive Christians. It has existed, to a greater or less extent, in the Church ever since. It is a mysterious fact often manifested in a most surprising manner. Sometimes a single sentence, a word, a gesture, or even a look will convey this power in an overcoming manner.

To the honor of God alone I will say a little of my own experience in this matter. I was powerfully converted on the morning of the 10th of October. In the evening of the same day, and on the morning of the following day, I received overwhelming baptisms of the Holy Ghost, that went through me, as it seemed to me, body and soul. I immediately found myself endued with such power from on high that a few words dropped here and there to individuals were the means of their immediate conversion. My words seemed to fasten like barbed arrows in the souls of men. They cut like a sword. They broke the heart like a hammer. Multitudes can attest to this. Oftentimes a word dropped, without my remembering it, would fasten conviction, and often result in almost immediate conversion. Sometimes I would find myself, in a great measure, empty of this power. I would go out and visit, and find that I made no saving impression. I would exhort and pray, with the same result. I would then set apart a day for private fasting and prayer, fearing that this power had departed from me, and would inquire anxiously after the reason of this apparent emptiness. After humbling myself, and crying out for help, the power would return upon me with all its freshness. This has been the experience of my life.

I could fill a volume with the history of my own experience and observation with respect to this power from on high. It is a fact of consciousness and of observation, but a great mystery. I have said that sometimes a look has in it the power of God. I have often witnessed this. Let the following fact illustrate it. I once preached, for the first time, in a mill town. The next morning I went into the manufacturing establishment to view its operations. As I passed into the weaving department I beheld a great company of young women, some of whom, I observed, were looking at me, and then on each other, in a manner that indicated a frivolous spirit, and that they knew me. I, however, knew none of them. As I approached nearer to those who had recognized me they seemed to increase in their manifestations of lightness of mind. Their levity made a peculiar impression upon me; I felt it in my heart. I stopped short and looked at them, I know not how, as my whole mind was absorbed with the sense of their guilt and danger. As I steadily looked at them I observed that one of them became very much agitated. A thread broke. She attempted to mend it; but her hands trembled in such a manner that she could not do it. I immediately observed that the sensation was spreading, and had become universal among the group. I looked steadily at them until one after another gave up and paid no more attention to their looms. They fell on their knees, and the influence spread throughout the whole room. I had not spoken a word; and the noise of the looms would have prevented my being heard if I had. In a few minutes all work was abandoned, and tears and lamentations filled the room. At this moment the owner of the factory, who was himself an unconverted man, came in, accompanied, I believe, by the superintendent who was a professed Christian. When the owner saw the state of things he said to the superintendent, "Stop the mill." What he saw seemed to pierce him to the heart.

"It is more important, " he hurriedly remarked, "that these souls should be saved than that this mill should run." As soon as the noise of the machinery had ceased, the owner inquired: "What shall we do? We must have a place to meet, where we can receive instruction." The superintendent replied: "The mule room will do." The mules were run up out of the way, and all of the hands were notified and assembled in that room. We had a marvelous meeting. I prayed with them and gave them such instruction as at the time they could bear. The word was with power. Many expressed hope that day; and within a few days, as I was informed, nearly every person in that great establishment, together with the owner, had hope in Christ.

This power is a great marvel. I have many times seen people unable to endure the word. The most simple and ordinary statement would cut men off from their seats like a sword, would take away their bodily strength and render them almost as helpless as dead men. Several times it has been true in my experience that I could not raise my voice, or say anything in prayer or exhortation except in the mildest manner, without wholly overcoming those who were present. This was not because I was preaching terror to the people; but the sweetest sounds of the gospel would overcome them. This power seems sometimes to pervade the atmosphere of one who is highly charged with it. Many times great numbers of persons in a community will be clothed with this power, when the very atmosphere of the whole place seems to be charged with the life of God. Strangers coming into it and passing through the place will be instantly smitten with conviction of sin, and in many instances converted to Christ. When Christians humble themselves and consecrate their all afresh to Christ, and ask for this power, they will often receive such a baptism that they will be instrumental in converting more souls in one day than in all their lifetime before. While Christians remain humble enough to retain this power the work of conversion will go on, till whole communities and regions of country are converted to Christ. The same is true of ministers. But this article is long enough. If you will allow me, I shall have more to say upon this subject.

3

The Enduement of the Spirit

Since the publication in the *Independent* of my article on "The Power from on High" I have been confined with a prolonged illness. In the meantime I have received numerous letters of inquiry upon the subject. They relate mostly to three particular points of inquiry:

1. They request further illustrations of the exhibition of this power.

2. They inquire, "Who have a right to expect this enduement?"

3. "How or upon what conditions can it be obtained?"

I am unable to answer these inquiries by letters to individuals. With your leave I propose, if my health continues to improve, to reply to them in several short articles through your columns. In the present number I will relate another exhibition of this power from on high, as witnessed by myself.

Soon after I was licensed to preach I went into a region of the country where I was an entire stranger. I went there at the request of a Female Missionary Society, located in Oneida County, New York. Early in May, I think, I visited the town of Antwerp, in the northern part of Jefferson County. I stopped at the village hotel, and there learned that there were no religious meetings held in that town at that time. They had a brick meetinghouse, but it was locked up. By personal efforts I got a few people to assemble in the living room of a Christian lady in the place, and I preached to them on the evening after my arrival. As I walked around the village I was shocked with the horrible profanity that I heard among the men wherever I went. I obtained permission to preach in the schoolhouse on the next Sunday; but before that Sunday arrived I was much discouraged, and almost terrified, in view of the state of society which I witnessed. On Saturday the Lord applied with power to my heart the following words, addressed by the Lord Jesus to Paul (Acts 18:9,10): "Be not afraid, but speak, and hold not thy peace; for I am with thee, and no man shall set on thee to hurt thee; for I have much people in this city." This completely subdued my fears; but my heart was loaded with agony for the people.

On Sunday morning I rose early and retired to

a grove not far from the village to pour out my heart before God for a blessing on the labors of the day. I could not express the agony of my soul in words, but struggled with much groaning and, I believe, with many tears, for an hour or two, without getting relief. I returned to my room in the hotel; but almost immediately came back to the grove. This I did three times. The last time I got complete relief, just as it was time to go to the meeting. I went to the schoolhouse and found it filled to its capacity. I took out my little pocket Bible and read for my text: "God so loved the world that He gave His only begotten Son, that whosoever believeth in Him should not perish, but have everlasting life." I set forth the love of God as contrasted with the manner in which He was treated by those for whom He gave up His Son. I charged home their profanity upon them; and as I recognized among my hearers several whose profanity I had particularly noticed, in the fullness of my heart and the flowing of my tears I pointed to them and said, "I heard these men call upon God to damn their fellows." The Word took powerful effect. Nobody seemed offended, but almost everybody greatly melted.

At the close of the service the amiable landlord, Mr. Copeland, rose and said he would open the meetinghouse in the afternoon. He did so. The meetinghouse was full and, as in the morning, the Word took powerful effect. Thus a powerful revival commenced in the village, which soon after spread in every direction.

I think it was on the second Sunday after this, when I came out of the pulpit in the afternoon, an aged man approached and said to me: "Can you not come and preach in our neighborhood? We have never had any religious meetings there." I inquired the direction and the distance, and made an appointment to preach there the next afternoon, Monday, at five o'clock, in their school-house. I had preached three times in the village and attended two prayer meetings on the Lord's Day, and on Monday I went on foot to fulfill this appointment. As the weather was very warm that day I felt almost too weary to walk and I was greatly discouraged before I arrived. I sat down in the shade by the wayside and felt as if I was too faint to continue. I felt, if I did, I was too discouraged to talk to the people. When I finally arrived I found the house to be filled and immediately started the service with a hymn. The people attempted to sing, but the horrible discord agonized me beyond expression. I leaned forward, put my elbows upon my knees and my hands over my ears and shook my head to shut out the discord, which I could barely endure. As soon as they had stopped singing I got on my knees, almost in a state of desperation. The Lord opened the windows of heaven upon me and gave me great enlargement and power in prayer.

Up to this moment I had no idea what text I should use on the occasion. As I rose from my knees the Lord gave me this: "Up, get you out of this place, for the Lord will destroy this city." I told the people, as nearly as I could recollect, where they would find it, and went on to tell them of the destruction of Sodom. I gave them an outline of the history of Abraham and Lot, and their relations to each other; of Abraham's praying for Sodom, and of Lot, as the only pious man that was found in the city. While I was doing this I was struck with the fact that the people looked exceedingly angry about me. Many countenances appeared very threatening, and some of the men looked as if they were about to strike me. This I could not understand, as I was only giving them, with great liberty of spirit, some interesting sketches of Bible history. As soon as I had completed the historical sketch I turned upon them and said that I had understood they had never had any religious meetings in that neighborhood. I then applied that fact as I thrust at them with the sword of the Spirit with all my might. From this moment the solemnity increased with great rapidity. In a few moments there seemed to fall upon the congregation an instantaneous shock. I cannot describe the sensation that I felt, nor that which was apparent in the congregation; but the word seemed *literally* to cut like a sword. The power from on high came down upon them in such a torrent that they fell from their seats in every direction. In less than a minute nearly all the congregation were either down on their knees or on their faces, or in *some* position prostrate before God. Everyone was crying or groaning for mercy upon his own soul. They paid no further attention to me or to my preaching. I tried to *get* their attention but I could not.

I observed the aged man who had invited me there as still retaining his seat near the center of the house. He was *staring* around him with unutterable astonishment. Pointing to him, I cried at the top of my voice, "Can't you *pray?*" He knelt down and roared out a short prayer about as loud as he could holler, but they paid no attention to him.

After looking around for a few moments, I knelt down and put my hand on the head of a young man who was kneeling at my feet, and engaged in prayer for mercy on his soul. I got his attention and preached Jesus in his ear. In a few moments he seized Jesus by faith, and then broke out in prayer for those around him. I then turned to another in the same way with the same result; and then another, and another, till I know not how many had laid hold of Christ and were full of prayer for others. After continuing in this way until nearly sunset I was obliged to commit the meeting to the charge of the old gentleman who had invited me, as I had to go to fulfill an appointment in another place in the evening.

In the afternoon of the next day I was requested to hurry back to this place, as they had not been able to break up the meeting. They had been obliged to leave the schoolhouse to give place to the school, but they had moved to a private house nearby. There I found a number of persons still too anxious and too much loaded down with conviction to go to their homes. These were soon subdued by the Word of God, and I believe all obtained a hope before they went home.

Observe, I was a total stranger in that place. I had never seen nor heard of it before this time. However, here at my second visit, I learned that the place was called Sodom by reason of its wickedness; and the old man who invited me was called Lot because he was the only person professing faith in Christ in that place.

After this manner the revival broke out in this neighborhood.

I have not been in that neighborhood for many years; but in 1856, I think, while laboring in Syracuse, New York, I was introduced to a minister of Christ from St. Lawrence County by the name of Cross. He said to me, "Mr. Finney, you don't know me, but do you remember preaching in a place called Sodom?" I said, "I shall never forget it." He replied, "I was then a young man, and was converted at that meeting." He is still living, a pastor in one of the churches in that county, and is the father of the principal of our preparatory department. Those who have lived in that region can testify of the permanent results of that blessed revival. I can only give in words a *feeble* description of that wonderful manifestation of power from on high attending the preaching of the Word.

4

The Enduement of Power From on High

In this article I propose to consider the conditions upon which this enduement of power can be obtained. Let us borrow a little light from the Scriptures. I will not encumber your paper with quotations from the Bible, but simply state a few facts that will readily be recognized by all readers of the Scriptures. If the readers of this article will read in the last chapter of Matthew and of Luke the commission which Christ gave to His disciples, and in connection read the first and second chapters of the Acts of the Apostles, they will be prepared to appreciate what I have to say in this article.

1st. The disciples had already been converted to Christ, and their faith had been confirmed by

His resurrection. But here let me say that conversion to Christ is not to be confounded with a consecration to the great work of the world's conversion. In conversion the soul has to do directly and personally with Christ. It yields up its prejudices, its selfishness; accepts Him, trusts Him, and supremely loves Him. All this the disciples had, more or less, distinctly done. But as yet they had received no definite commission, and no particular enduement of power to fulfill a commission.

2nd. But when Christ had dispelled their great bewilderment resulting from His crucifixion, and confirmed their faith by repeated interviews with them, He gave them their great commission to win all nations to Himself. But He admonished them to tarry at Jerusalem until they were endued with power from on high, which He said they should receive not many days hence. Now observe what they did. They assembled, the men and women, for prayer. They accepted the commission, and, doubtless, came to an understanding of the *nature* of the commission and the necessity of the spiritual enduement which Christ had promised. As they continued day after day in prayer and self-examination they, no doubt, came to appreciate more and more the difficulties that would beset them, and to feel more and more their inadequacy to the task. A consideration of the circumstances and results leads to the conclusion that they, one and all, consecrated themselves with all they had to the conversion of the world as their life work. They must have renounced utterly the idea of living to themselves in any form, and devoted themselves with all their powers to the work set before them. This consecration of themselves to the work, this self-renunciation, this dying to all that the world could offer them, must, in the order of nature, have preceded their intelligent seeking of the promised enduement of power from on high. They then continued, with one accord, in prayer for the promised baptism of the Spirit, which baptism included all that was essential to their success. Observe, they had a work set before them. They had a promise of power to perform it. They were admonished to wait until the promise was fulfilled. How did they wait? Not in listlessness and inactivity; not in making preparations by study and otherwise to get along without it; not by going about their business and offering an occasional prayer that the promise might be fulfilled; but they *continued* in prayer, and persisted in their petitions until the answer came. They understood that it was to be a baptism of the Holy Ghost. They understood that it was to be received from Christ. They prayed in faith. They held on, with the firmest expectation, until the enduement came. Now, let these facts instruct us as to the conditions of receiving this enduement of power.

1. We, as Christians, have the same commission to fulfill. As truly as they did, we need an enduement of power from on high. Of course, the same injunction, to wait upon God until we receive

it, is given to us.

2. We have the same promise that they had. Now, let us take substantially and in spirit the same course that they did. They were Christians, and had a measure of the Spirit to lead them in prayer and in consecration. So have we. Every Christian possesses a measure of the Spirit of Christ, enough of the Holy Spirit to lead us to true consecration and inspire us with the faith that is essential to our prevalence in prayer. Let us, then, not grieve or resist Him: but accept the commission, fully consecrate ourselves, with all we have, to the saving of souls as our great and our only lifework. Let us go to the altar with all we have and are, and lie there and persist in prayer until we receive the enduement. Now, observe, conversion to Christ is not to be confounded with the acceptance of this commission to convert the world. The first is a personal transaction between the soul and Christ relating to its own salvation. The second is the soul's acceptance of the service in which Christ proposes to employ it. Christ does not require us to make brick without straw. To whom He gives the commission He also gives the admonition and the promise. If the commission is heartily accepted, if the promise is believed, if the admonition to wait upon the Lord until our strength is renewed be complied with, we shall receive the enduement.

3. It is of supreme importance that all Christians should understand that this commission to convert the world is given to them by Christ

individually.

Everyone has the great responsibility devolved upon him or her to win as many souls as possible to Christ. This is the great privilege and the great duty of all the disciples of Christ. There are a great many departments in this work. But in every department we may and ought to possess this power so that, whether we preach or pray, or write, or print, or trade, or travel, take care of children, or administer the government of the state, or whatever we do, our whole life and influence should be permeated with this power. Christ says: "If any man believe in Me, out of his inmost being shall flow rivers of living water"— that is, a Christian influence having in it the element of power to impress the truth of Christ upon the hearts of men, shall proceed from Him. The great need of the Church at present is, first, the clear conviction that this commission to convert the world is given to each of Christ's disciples as his lifework. I fear I must say that the great mass of professing Christians seem never to have been impressed with this truth. The work of saving souls they leave to ministers.

The second great need is a clear conviction of the necessity of this enduement of power upon every individual soul. Many professing Christians suppose it belongs especially and only to such as are called to preach the gospel as a lifework. They fail to realize that all are called to preach the gospel, that the whole life of every Christian is to be a proclamation of the glad tidings.

A third need is an earnest faith in the promise of this enduement. A great many professing Christians, and even ministers, seem to doubt whether this promise is to the whole Church and to every Christian. Consequently, they have no faith to lay hold of it. If it does not belong to all, they don't know to whom it does belong. So naturally they cannot lay hold of the promise by faith.

A fourth need is persistence in waiting upon God for the power, as is enjoined in the Scriptures. They faint before they have prevailed, and hence the enduement is not received. Multitudes seem to satisfy themselves with a hope of eternal life for themselves. They never get ready to move beyond the question of their own salvation, leaving that as settled with Christ. They don't get ready to accept the great commission to work for the salvation of others, because their faith is so weak that they do not steadily leave the question of their own salvation in the hands of Christ; and even some ministers of the gospel, I find, are in the same condition, and halting in the same way, unable to give themselves wholly to the work of saving others because in a measure unsettled about their own salvation.

It is amazing to witness the extent to which the Church has practically lost sight of the necessity of this enduement of power. Much is said of our dependence upon the Holy Spirit by almost everybody; but how little is this dependence realized. Christians and even ministers go to work without it. I mourn to be obliged to say that the ranks of the ministry seem to be filling up with those who do not possess it. May the Lord have mercy upon us! Will this last remark be thought uncharitable? If so, let the report of the Home Missionary Society, for example, be heard upon this subject. Surely, something is wrong.

An average of five souls won to Christ by each missionary of that Society in a year's toil certainly indicates a most alarming weakness in the ministry. Have all or even a majority of these ministers been endued with the power which Christ promised? If not, why not? But if they have, is this all that Christ intended by His promise? In a former article I have said that the reception of this enduement of power is instantaneous. I do not mean to assert that in every instance the recipient was aware of the precise time at which the power commenced to work mightily within him. It may have commenced like the dew and increased to a shower. I have alluded to the report of the Home Missionary Society. Not that I suppose that the brethren employed by that Society are exceptionally weak in faith and power as laborers for God. On the contrary, from my acquaintance with some of them I regard them among our most devoted and self-denying laborers in the cause of God. This fact illustrates the alarming weakness that pervades every branch of the Church, both clergy and laity. Are we not weak? Are we not criminally weak? It has been suggested that by writing thus I would offend the ministry and the Church. I cannot believe that the statement of so palpable a fact will be regarded as an offense. The fact is, there is something sadly defective in the education of the ministry and of the Church. The ministry is weak because the Church is weak. And then, again, the Church is kept weak by the weakness of the ministry. Oh for a conviction of the necessity of this enduement of power and faith in the promise of Christ!

5

Is It a Hard Saying?

In a former article I said that the lack of an enduement of power from on high should be deemed a disqualification for a pastor, a deacon or elder, a Sunday School superintendent, a professor in a Christian college, and especially for a professor in a theological seminary. Is this a hard saying? Is this an uncharitable saying? Is it unjust? Is it unreasonable? Is it unscriptural? Suppose any one of the apostles, or those present on the day of Pentecost, had failed through apathy, selfishness, unbelief, indolence, or ignorance to obtain this enduement of power, would it have been uncharitable, unjust, unreasonable, or unscriptural, to have accounted him disqualified for the work which Christ had appointed them?

Christ had expressly informed them that without this enduement they could do nothing. He had expressly enjoined it upon them not to attempt it in their own strength, but to tarry at Jerusalem until they received the necessary power from on high. He had also expressly promised that if they tarried, in the sense which He intended, they should receive it "not many days hence." They evidently understood Him to enjoin upon them to tarry in the sense of a constant waiting upon Him in prayer and supplication for the blessing. Now, suppose that any one of them had stayed away and attended to his own business, and waited for the sovereignty of God to confer this power. He of course would have been disqualified for the work; and if his fellow-Christians, who had obtained this power, had deemed him so, would it have been uncharitable, unreasonable, unscriptural?

And is it not true of all to whom the command to disciple the world is given, and to whom the promise of this power is made, if through any shortcoming or fault of theirs they fail to obtain this gift that they are in fact disqualified for the work, and especially for any official station? Are they not, in fact, disqualified for leadership in the sacramental host? Are they qualified as teachers of those who are to do the work? If it is a fact that they do lack this power, however this defect is to be accounted for, it is also a fact that they are not qualified to be teachers of God's people; and if they are seen to be disqualified because they lack this power, it must

be reasonable and right and scriptural so to deem
them, and so to speak of them, and so to treat
them. Who has a right to complain? Surely they
have not. Shall the Church of God be burdened
with teachers and leaders who lack this fundamental qualification, when their failing to possess it
must be their own fault? The manifest apathy,
indolence, ignorance, and unbelief that exists upon
this subject is truly amazing. They are inexcusable.
They must be highly criminal. With such a command to convert the world ringing in our ears; with
such an injunction to wait in constant, wrestling
prayer until we receive the power; with such a
promise, made by such a Savior, held out to us of
all the help we need from Christ Himself, what
excuse can we offer for being powerless in this
great work? What an awful responsibility rests
upon us, upon the whole Church, upon every
Christian!

One might ask, How is apathy, how is indolence, how is the common fatal neglect possible
under such circumstances? If any of the primitive
Christians to whom this commandment was given
had failed to receive this power, should we not
think them greatly to blame? If such default had
been sin in them, how much more in us with all the
light of history and of fact blazing upon us, which
they had not received? Some ministers and many
Christians treat this matter as if it were to be left to
the sovereignty of God, without any persistent
effort to obtain this enduement. Did the primitive

Christians so understand and treat it? No, indeed. They gave themselves no rest until this baptism of power came upon them.

I once heard a minister preaching upon the subject of the baptism of the Holy Ghost. He treated it as a reality; and when he came to the question of how it was to be obtained, he said truly that it was to be obtained as the apostles obtained it on the day of Pentecost. I was much gratified, and listened eagerly to hear him press the obligation on his hearers to give themselves no rest until they had obtained it. But in this I was disappointed: for before he sat down he seemed to relieve the audience from the feeling of obligation to obtain the baptism and left the impression that the matter was to be left to the discretion of God, and said what appeared to imply a censure of those that vehemently and persistently urged upon God the fulfillment of the promise. Neither did he hold out to them the certainty of their obtaining the blessing if they fulfilled the conditions. The sermon was in most respects a good one; but I think the audience left without any feeling of encouragement or sense of obligation to seek earnestly the baptism. This is a common fault of the sermons that I hear. There is much that is instructive in them; but they fail to leave either a sense of obligation or a feeling of great encouragement, as to the use of means, upon the congregation. They are greatly defective in their winding up. They neither leave the conscience under a pressure nor the whole mind under the stimulus of hope. The doctrine is often good, but the "what then?" is often left out.

Many ministers and professors of religion seem to be theorizing, criticizing, and endeavoring to justify their neglect of this attainment. So did not the apostles and other Christians. It was not a question which they endeavored to grasp with their intellects before they embraced it with their hearts. It was with them, as it should be with us, a question of *faith* in a *promise*. I find many persons endeavoring to grasp with their intellect and settle as a theory questions of pure experience. They are puzzling themselves with endeavors to apprehend with the intellect that which is to be received as a conscious experience through faith.

There is need of a great reformation in the Church on this particular point. The churches should wake up to the facts in the case and take a new position, a firm stand in regard to the qualifications of ministers and church officers. They should refuse to settle on a man as pastor of whose qualifications for the office in this respect they are not well satisfied. Whatever else he may have to recommend him, if his record does not show that he has this enduement of power to win souls to Christ, they should deem him unqualified. It used to be the custom of churches, and I believe in some places is so still, in presenting a call to the pastorate, to certify that having witnessed the spiritual fruits of his labors they deem him qualified and called of God to the work of the ministry. Churches should be well satisfied in some way that they call a *fruitful* minister and not a dry stalk — that is, a mere intellect, a mere head with little heart; an elegant writer, but with no unction; a great logician, but of little faith; a fervid imagination, it may be, but with no Holy Ghost power.

The churches should hold the theological seminaries to a strict account in this matter; and until they do, I fear the theological seminaries will never wake up to their responsibility. Some years ago, one branch of the Scottish Church was so disturbed with the lack of unction and power in the ministers furnished them by their theological seminary that they passed a resolution that until the seminary reformed in this respect they would not employ ministers that were educated there. This was a necessary, a just, a timely rebuke, which I believe had a very salutary effect. A theological seminary ought by all means to be a school not merely for the teaching of doctrine, but also, and even more especially, for the development of Christian experience. To be sure, the intellect should be well furnished in those schools; but it is immeasurably more important that the pupils should be led to a thorough personal knowledge of Christ, and the power of His resurrection, and the fellowship of His sufferings, and to be made conformable to His death. A theological seminary that aims mainly at the culture of the intellect, and sends out learned men who lack this enduement of power from on high, is a snare and a stumbling block to the Church. The seminaries should recommend no one to the churches, however great his intellectual attainments, unless he has this most essential of all attainments, the enduement of power from on high. The seminaries should be held as incompetent to educate men for the ministry if it is seen that they send out men as ministers who have not this most essential qualification. The churches should inform themselves, and look to those seminaries which furnish not merely the best educated but the most unctuous and spiritually powerful ministers.

It is amazing that while it is generally admitted that the enduement of power from on high is a reality, and essential to ministerial success, practically it should be treated by the churches and by the schools as of comparatively little importance. In theory it is admitted to be everything, but in practice treated as if it were nothing. From the apostles to the present day it has been seen that men of very little human culture, but endued with this power, have been highly successful in winning souls to Christ; while men of the greatest learning, with all that the schools have done for them, have been powerless so far as the proper work of the ministry is concerned. And yet we go on laying ten times more stress on human culture than we do on the baptism of the Holy Ghost. Practically, human culture is treated as infinitely more important than the enduement of power high.

Most seminaries are furnished with learned men, but often not with men of spiritual power; hence, they do not insist upon this enduement of power as indispensable to the work of the ministry. Students are pressed almost beyond endurance with study and the culture of the intellect while scarcely an hour in a day is given to instruction in Christian experience. Indeed, I do not know that so much as one course of lectures on Christian experience is given in the theological seminaries. But religion is an experience. It is a consciousness. Personal fellowship with God is the secret of the whole of it. There is a world of most essential learning in this direction wholly neglected by the theological seminaries. With them doctrine, philosophy, theology, Church history, sermonizing are everything, and real heartunion with God nothing. Spiritual power to prevail with God and to prevail with man has but little place in their teaching.

I have often been surprised at the judgment men form in regard to the prospective usefulness of young men preparing for the ministry. Even professors are very apt, I see, to deceive themselves on this subject. If a young man is a good scholar, a fine writer, makes good progress in exegesis and stands high in intellectual culture, they have strong hopes for him, even though they must know in many such cases that these young men cannot pray — that they have no unction, no power in prayer, no spirit of wrestling, of agonizing and prevailing with God. Yet they are expecting them, because of their culture, to make their mark in the ministry, to be highly useful. For my part, I expect no such thing of this class of men. I have infinitely more hope for the usefulness of a man who, at any cost, will keep up daily fellowship with God; who is yearning for and struggling after the highest possible spiritual attainment; who will not live without daily prevalence in prayer and being clothed with power from on high. Churches, presbyteries, associations, and whoever license young men for the ministry are often very faulty in this respect. They will spend hours in informing themselves of the intellectual culture of the candidates, but scarcely as many minutes in ascertaining their heart culture — what they know of the power of Christ to save from sin, what they know of the power of prayer, and whether and to what extent they are endued with power from on high to win souls to Christ. The whole proceeding on such occasions cannot but leave the impression that human learning is preferred to spiritual unction. Oh that it were different, and that we were all agreed, practically, now and forever, to hold fast to the promise of Christ, and never think ourselves or anybody else to be fit for the great work of the Church until we have received a rich enduement of power from on high.

I beg of my brethren, and especially my younger brethren, not to conceive of these articles as written in the spirit of reproach. I beg the churches, I beg the seminaries, to receive a word of exhortation from an old man, who has had some experience in these things, and one whose heart mourns and is weighed down in view of the shortcomings of the Church, the ministers, and the seminaries on this subject. Brethren, I beseech you to more thoroughly consider this matter, to wake up and lay it to heart, and rest not until this subject of the enduement of power from on high is brought forward into its proper place and takes that prominent and practical position in the view of the whole Church that Christ intended it should.

6

Prevailing Prayer

Prevailing prayer is that which secures an answer. Saying prayers is not offering prevailing prayer. The effectiveness of prayer does not depend so much on quantity as on quality. I do not know how better to approach this subject than by relating a fact of my own experience before I was converted. I relate it because I fear such experiences are but too common among unconverted men.

I do not recollect having ever attended a prayer meeting until after I began the study of law. Then, for the first time, I lived in a neighborhood where there was a weekly prayer meeting. I had neither known, heard, nor seen much of religion; hence I had no settled opinions about it. Partly from curiosity and partly from an uneasiness of mind upon the subject, which I could not well define, I began to attend that prayer meeting. About the same time I bought the first Bible that I ever owned, and I began to read it. I listened to the prayers which I heard offered in those prayer meetings with all the attention that I could give to prayers so cold and formal. In every prayer they prayed for the gift and outpouring of the Holy Spirit. Both in their prayers and in their remarks, which were occasionally interspersed, they acknowledged that they did not prevail with God. This was most evident, and had almost made me a skeptic.

Seeing me so frequently in their prayer meeting, the leader, on one occasion, asked me if I did not wish them to pray for me. I replied, "No." I said, "I suppose that I need to be prayed for, but your prayers are not answered. You confess it yourselves." I then expressed my astonishment at this fact, in view of what the Bible said about the effectiveness of prayer. Indeed, for some time my mind was much perplexed and in doubt in view of Christ's teaching on the subject of prayer and the manifest facts before me, from week to week, in this prayer meeting. Was Christ a divine teacher? Did He actually teach what the Gospels attributed to Him? Did He mean what He said? Did prayer really avail to secure blessings from God? If so, what was I to make of what I witnessed from week to week and month to month in that prayer meeting? Were they real Christians? Was that which I heard *real prayer*, in the Bible sense? Was it such prayer as Christ had promised to answer? Here I found the solution.

I became convinced that they were under a delusion; that they did not prevail because they had no *right* to prevail. They did not comply with the conditions upon which God had promised to hear prayer. Their prayers were just such as God had promised *not* to answer. It was evident they were overlooking the fact that they were in danger of praying themselves into skepticism in regard to the value of prayer.

In reading my Bible I noticed such revealed conditions as the following:

(a) Faith in God as the answerer of prayer. This, it is plain, involves the expectation of receiving what we ask.

(b) Another revealed condition is the asking according to the revealed will of God. This plainly implies asking not only for such things as God is willing to grant, but also asking in such a state of mind as God can accept. I fear it is common for professed Christians to overlook the state of mind in which God requires them to be as a condition of answering their prayers.

For example: In offering the Lord's Prayer, "Thy kingdom come," it is plain that sincerity is a condition of prevailing with God. But sincerity in offering this petition implies the whole heart and life devotion of the petitioner to the building up of this kingdom. It implies the sincere and thorough consecration of all that we have and all that we are to this end. To utter this petition in any other state of mind involves hypocrisy and is an abomination.

So in the next petition, "Thy will be done on earth as it is in heaven." God has not promised to hear *this* petition unless it is sincerely offered. But *sincerity* implies a state of mind that accepts the whole revealed will of God, so far as we understand it, as they accept it in heaven. It implies a loving, confiding, universal obedience to the whole *known* will of God, whether that will is revealed in His Word, by His Spirit, or in His providence. It implies that we hold ourselves and all that we have and are as absolutely and cordially at God's disposal as do the inhabitants of heaven. If we fall short of this, and withhold anything whatsoever from God, we "regard iniquity in our hearts" and God will not hear us.

Sincerity in offering this petition implies a state of entire and universal consecration to God. Anything short of this is withholding from God that which is His due. It is "turning away our ear from hearing the law." But what saith the Scriptures? "He that turneth away his ear from hearing the law, even his prayer shall be an abomination." Do professed Christians understand this?

What is true of offering these two petitions is true of *all* prayer. Do Christians lay this to heart? Do they consider that all professed prayer is an abomination if it be not offered in a state of entire consecration of all that we have and are to God? If we do not offer ourselves with and in our prayers, with all that we have; if we are not in a state of mind that cordially accepts and, so far as we know, perfectly conforms to the whole will of God, our prayer is an abomination. How awfully profane is the use very frequently made of the Lord's Prayer, both in public and in private. To hear men and women chatter through the Lord's Prayer, "Thy kingdom come, Thy will be done on earth as it is in heaven," while their lives are anything but conformed to the known will of God is shocking and revolting. To hear men pray "Thy kingdom come" while it is most evident that they are making little or no sacrifice or effort to promote this kingdom, forces the conviction of bare-faced hypocrisy. Such is not prevailing prayer.

(c) Unselfishness is a condition of prevailing prayer. "Ye ask and receive not, because ye ask amiss, that ye may consume it upon your lusts" (James 4:3).

(d) Another condition of prevailing prayer is a conscience void of offence toward God and man. I John 3:20,22: "If our heart [conscience] condemn us, God is greater than our heart and knoweth all things; if our heart condemn us not, then have we confidence toward God, and whatsoever we ask we receive of Him, because we keep His commandments and do those things that are pleasing in His sight." Here two things are made plain: first, that to prevail with God we must keep a conscience void of offence; and second, that we must keep His commandments and do those things that are pleasing in His sight.

(e) A pure heart is also a condition of prevailing prayer. Psalm 66:18: "If I regard iniquity in my heart, the Lord will not hear me."

(f) All due confession and restitution to God and man is another condition of prevailing prayer. Proverbs 28:13: "He that covereth his sins shall not prosper. Whoso confesseth and forsaketh them shall find mercy."

(g) Clean hands is another condition. Psalm 26:6: "I will wash mine hands in innocency; so will I compass thine altar, O Lord." I Timothy 2:8: "I will that men pray everywhere, lifting up holy hands, without wrath and doubting."

(h) The settling of disputes and animosities among brethren is a condition. Matthew 5:23,24: "If thou bring thy gift to the altar, and there rememberest that thy brother hath aught against thee, leave there thy gift before the altar and go thy way. First be reconciled to thy brother, then come and offer thy gift."

(i) Humility is another condition of prevailing prayer. James 4:6: "God resisteth the proud, but giveth grace to the humble."

(j) Taking up the stumbling blocks is another condition. Ezekiel 14:3: "Son of man, these men have set up their idols in their heart, and put the stumbling block of their iniquity before their face. Should I be inquired of at all by them?"

(k) A forgiving spirit is a condition. Matthew 6:12: "Forgive us our debts as we forgive our debtors"; verse 15: "But if ye forgive not men their trespasses, neither will your Heavenly Father forgive your trespasses."

(l) The exercise of a truthful spirit is a condition. Psalm 51:6: "Behold, Thou desirest truth in the inward parts." If the heart be not in a truthful state, if it be not entirely sincere and unselfish, we regard iniquity in our hearts; and, therefore, the Lord will not hear us.

(m) Praying in the name of Christ in a condition of prevailing prayer.

(n)The inspiration of the Holy Spirit is another condition. All truly prevailing prayer is inspired by the Holy Ghost. Romans 8:26,27: "For we know not what we should pray for as we ought, but the Spirit Himself maketh intercession for us with groanings which cannot be uttered. And He that searcheth the heart knoweth what is the mind of the Spirit, because He maketh intercession for the saints according to the will of God." This is the true spirit of prayer. This is being led by the Spirit in prayer. It is the only really prevailing prayer. Do professed Christians really understand this? Do they believe that unless they live and walk in the Spirit, unless they are taught how to pray by the intercession of the Spirit in them, they cannot prevail with God?

(o) Fervency is a condition. A prayer, to be prevailing, must be fervent. James 5:16: "Confess your faults one to another, and pray one for another, that ye may be healed. The effectual fervent prayer of a righteous man availeth much."

(p) Perseverance or persistence in prayer is often a condition of prevailing. See the case of Jacob, of Daniel, of Elijah, of the Syrophenician woman, the parable of the unjust judge, and the teaching of the Bible generally.

(q) Travail of soul is often a condition of prevailing prayer. "As soon as Zion travailed, she brought forth her children." "My little children," said Paul, "for whom I travail in birth again, till Christ be formed in you." This implies that he had travailed in birth for them before they were converted. Indeed, travail of soul in prayer is the only real revival prayer. If anyone does not know what this is, he does not understand the spirit of prayer. He is not in a revival state. He does not understand the passage already quoted — Romans 8:26,27. Until he understands this agonizing prayer he does not know the real secret of revival power.

(r) Another condition of prevailing prayer is the consistent use of means to secure the object prayed for, if means are within our reach and are known by us to be necessary to the securing of the end. To pray for a revival of religion and use no other means is to tempt God. This, I could plainly see, was the case of those who offered prayer in the prayer meeting of which I have spoken. They continued to offer prayer for a revival of religion, but out of meeting they were as silent as death on the subject and opened not their mouths to those around them. They continued this inconsistency until a prominent impenitent man in the community administered to them in my presence a terrible rebuke. He expressed just what I deeply felt. He rose, and with the utmost solemnity and tearfulness said: "Christian people, what can you mean? You continue to pray in these meetings for a revival of religion. You often exhort each other here to wake up and use means to promote a revival. You assure each other, and assure us who are impenitent, that we are in the way to hell; and I believe it. You also insist that if you should wake up, and use the appropriate means, there would be a revival and we should be converted. You tell us of our great danger, and that our souls are worth more than all worlds; and yet you keep busy in your comparatively trifling employments and use no such means. We have no revival and our souls are not saved." Here he broke down and fell, sobbing, back into his seat. This rebuke fell heavily upon that prayer meeting, as I shall ever remember. It did them good; for it was not long before the members of that prayer meeting broke down, and we had a revival. I was present in the first meeting in which the revival spirit was manifest. Oh, how changed was the tone of their prayers, confessions, and supplications. I remarked, in returning home, to a friend: "What a change has come over these Christians. This must be the beginning of a revival." Yes, a wonderful change comes over all the meetings whenever the Christian people are revived. Then their confessions mean something. They mean reformation and restitution. They mean work. They mean the use of means. They mean the opening of their pockets, their hearts and hands, and the devotion of all their powers to the promotion of the work.

(s) Prevailing prayer is specific. It is offered for a definite object. We cannot prevail for everything at once. In all the cases recorded in the Bible in which prayer was answered, it is noteworthy that the petitioner prayed for a definite object.

(t) Another condition of prevailing prayer is that we mean what we say in prayer — that we make no false pretenses; in short, that we are entirely childlike and sincere, speaking out of the heart, saying nothing more nor less than we mean, feel, and believe.

(u) Another condition of prevailing prayer is a state of mind that assumes the good faith of God in all His promises.

(v) Another condition is "watching unto prayer" as well as "praying in the Holy Ghost." By this I mean guarding against everything that can quench or grieve the Spirit of God in our hearts. Also watching for the answer, in a state of mind that will diligently use all necessary means, at any expense, and add entreaty to entreaty.

When the fallow ground is thoroughly broken up in the hearts of Christians, when they have confessed and made restitution — if the work be thorough and honest — they will naturally and inevitably fulfill the conditions and will prevail in prayer. But it cannot be too distinctly understood that *none others will.* What we commonly hear in prayer and conference meetings is not prevailing prayer. It is often astonishing and lamentable to witness the delusions that prevail upon the subject. Who that has witnessed real revivals of religion has not been struck with the change that comes over the whole spirit and manner of the prayers of really revived Christians? I do not think I ever could have been converted if I had not discovered the solution to the question: "Why is it that so much that is called prayer is not answered?"

7

How to Win Souls

"Take heed unto thyself, and unto the doctrine; continue in them: for in doing this thou shalt both save thyself and them that hear thee" — 1 Tim. 4:16.

I beg leave in this article to suggest to my younger brethren in the ministry some thoughts on the philosophy of so preaching the gospel as to secure the salvation of souls. They are the result of much study, much prayer for divine teaching, and a practical experience of many years.

I understand the admonition at the head of this article to relate to the *matter, order,* and *manner* of preaching.

The problem is, How shall we win souls wholly to Christ? Certainly we must win them away from *themselves.*

1st. They are free moral agents, of course — rational, accountable.

2nd. They are in *rebellion against God,* wholly *alienated,* intensely *prejudiced,* and *committed* against Him.

3rd. They are committed to *self-gratification* as the end of their being.

4th. This committed *state* is moral depravity, the fountain of sin within them, from which flow by a natural law all their sinful ways. This committed voluntary state is their "wicked heart." This it is that needs a *radical change.*

5th. God is infinitely benevolent, and unconverted sinners are supremely selfish, so that they are *radically opposed* to God. Their committal to the gratification of their appetites and propensities is known in Bible language as "the carnal mind"; or, as in the margin, "the minding of the flesh," which is enmity against God.

6th. This enmity is voluntary, and must be overcome, if at all, by the Word of God, made effectual by the *teaching* of the Holy Spirit.

7th. The gospel is adapted to this end and, when wisely presented, we may confidently expect the effectual co-operation of the Holy Spirit. This is implied in our commission, "Go and disciple all nations, and lo! I am with you always, even to the end of the world."

8th. If we are unwise, illogical, unphilosophical, and out of all natuaral order in presenting the gospel, we have no warrant for expecting divine co-operation.

9th. In winning souls, as in everything else, God works through and in accordance with natural laws. Hence, if we would win souls we must wisely adapt means to this end. We must present the necessary truths and do so in that order adapted to the natural laws of mind, of thought and mental action. A false mental philosophy will greatly mislead us, and we shall often be found ignorantly working against the agency of the Holy Spirit.

10th. Sinners must be convicted of their enmity. They do not know God, and consequently are often ignorant of the opposition of their hearts to Him. "By the law is the knowledge of sin," because by the law the sinner gets his first true idea of God. By the law he first learns that God is perfectly benevolent, and infinitely opposed to all selfishness. This law, then, should be arrayed in all its majesty against the selfishness and enmity of the sinner.

11th. This law carries irresistible conviction of its righteousness, and no moral agent can doubt it.

12th. All men know that they have sinned, but not all are *convicted* of the *guilt* and *deserved punishment* of sin. The many are careless and do not feel the burden of sin, the horrors and terrors of remorse, and have not a sense of condemnation and of being lost.

13th. But without this they cannot understand or appreciate the gospel method of salvation. One cannot *intelligently* and *heartily* ask or accept a pardon until he sees and feels the *fact* and *justice* of his condemnation.

14th. It is absurd to suppose that a careless, unconvicted sinner can *intelligently* and *thankfully* accept the gospel offer of pardon until he accepts the righteousness of God in his condemnation. Conversion to Christ is an intelligent change. Hence the conviction of deserved punishment must precede the acceptance of mercy; for without this conviction the soul does not understand its need of mercy and, of course, the offer is rejected. The gospel is no glad tidings to the careless, unconvicted sinner.

15th. The spirituality of the law should be unsparingly applied to the conscience until the sinner's self-righteousness is annihilated, and he stands speechless and self-condemned before a holy God.

16th. In some men this conviction is already ripe, and the preacher may at once present Christ, with the hope of His being accepted; but at ordinary times such cases are exceptional. The great mass of sinners are careless, unconvicted, and to assume their conviction and preparedness to receive Christ, and, hence, to urge sinners immediately to accept Him, is to begin at the wrong end of our work — to render our teaching unintelligible. And such a course will be found to have been a mistaken one, whatever present appearances and professions may indicate. The sinner may obtain a hope under such teaching; but, unless the Holy Spirit supplies something which the preacher has failed to do, it will be found to be a false one. All the essential links of truth must be supplied.

17th. When the law has done its work, annihilated self-righteousness and shut the sinner up to the acceptance of mercy, he should be made to understand the moral impossibility of a just God dispensing with the execution of the penalty when the precept of law has been violated.

18th. Right here the sinner should be made to understand that from the benevolence of God he cannot justly infer that God can consistently forgive him. For unless public justice can be satisfied, the law of universal benevolence forbids the forgiveness of sin. If public justice is not regarded in the exercise of mercy, the good of the *public* is sacrificed to that of the *individual*. God will never do this.

19th. This teaching will shut the sinner up to look for some offering to *public* justice.

20th. Now give him the atonement as a fact *revealed* and shut him up to Christ as his own sin offering. Press the *revealed fact* that God has accepted the death of Christ as a substitute for the sinner's death, and that this is to be received upon the *testimony* of God.

21st. Being already crushed into contrition by the convicting power of the law, the revelation of the love of God manifested in the death of Christ will naturally beget great self-loathing and that godly sorrow that needs not to be repented of. Under this showing the sinner can never forgive himself. God is holy and glorious; and he a sinner, saved by sovereign grace. This teaching may be more or less formal as the souls you address are more or less thoughtful, intelligent, and able to understand.

22nd. It was not by accident that the dispensation of law preceded the dispensation of grace; but it is in the natural order of things, in accordance with established mental laws, and evermore the law must prepare the way for the gospel. To overlook this in instructing souls is almost certain to result in false hope, the introduction of a false standard of Christian experience, and to fill the Church with spurious converts. Time will make this plain.

23rd. The truth should be preached to the persons present, and so personally applied as to compel everyone to feel that you mean *him* or *her*. As has been often said of a certain preacher: "He does not preach, but explains clearly what other people preach, and seems to be talking directly to *me*."

24th. This course will rivet attention and cause your hearers to lose sight of the length of your sermon. They will tire if they feel no *personal* interest in what you say. To secure their individual interest in what you are saying is an indispensable condition of their being converted. And while their individual interest is thus awakened and held fast to your subject, they will seldom complain of the length of your sermon. In nearly all cases, if the people complain of the length of our sermons it is because we fail to interest them *personally* in what we have to say.

25th. If we fail to interest them personally it is either because we do not address them personally, because we lack unction and earnestness, because we lack clearness and force, or because we lack something else that we ought to possess. To make them feel that we and that God means *them* is indispensable.

26th. Do not think that earnest piety alone can make you successful in winning souls. This is only one condition of success. There must be common sense, there must be spiritual wisdom in adapting means to the end. Matter and manner and order and time and place all need to be wisely adjusted to the end we have in view.

27th. God may sometimes convert souls by men who are not spiritually minded, when they possess that natural sagacity which enables them to adapt means to that end; but the Bible warrants us in affirming that these are exceptional cases. Yet without this sagacity and the adaptation of means to this end, even a *spiritual* mind will fail to win souls to Christ.

28th. Souls need instruction in accordance with the measure of their intelligence. A few simple truths, when wisely applied and illuminated by the Holy Spirit, will convert children to Christ. I say *wisely* applied, for they too are sinners, and need the application of the law, as a schoolmaster, to bring them to Christ, that they may be justified by faith. It will sooner or later appear that supposed conversions to Christ are spurious where the preparatory law work has been omitted, and Christ has not been embraced as a Saviour from sin and condemnation.

29th. Sinners of education and culture, who are, perhaps as a result, unconvicted and skeptical in their hearts, need a vastly more extended and thorough application of truth. Professional men need the gospel net to be thrown quite around them, with no break through which they can escape; and, when thus dealt with, they are all the more sure to be converted in proportion to their real intelligence. I have found that a course of lectures addressed to lawyers, and adapted to their habits of thought and reasoning, is most *sure* to convert them.

30th. To be successful in winning souls we need to be observing — to study individual character, to press the facts of experience, observation, and revelation upon the consciences of all classes.

31st. Be sure to explain the terms you use. Before I was converted, I failed to hear the terms repentance, faith, regeneration, and conversion intelligibly explained. Repentance was described as a feeling. Faith was represented as an *intellectual* act or state and not as a *voluntary* act of *trust*. Regeneration was represented as some physical change in the *nature*, produced by the *direct power* of the Holy Spirit, instead of a *voluntary* change of the *ultimate preference* of the soul, produced by the spiritual *illumination* of the Holy Spirit. Conversion also was represented as being so completely the work of the Holy Spirit that the fact that it is the sinner's own act, under the *persuasions* of the Holy Spirit, was covered up.

32nd. Urge the fact that repentance involves the voluntary and actual renunciation of all sin; that it is a radical change of mind toward God.

33rd. Also the fact that saving faith is *heart trust* in Christ; that it works by love, it purifies the heart, and overcomes the world; that no faith is saving that has not these attributes.

34th. The sinner is required to put forth certain *mental acts*. What these are he needs to understand. Error in mental philosophy only embarrasses, and may fatally deceive the inquiring soul. Sinners are often put upon a wrong track. They are put under a strain to *feel* instead of putting forth the required acts of *will*. Before my conversion I never received from *man* any intelligible idea of the mental acts that God required of me.

35th. The deceitfulness of sin renders the inquiring soul exceedingly exposed to delusion; therefore it behooves teachers to beat about every bush, and to search out every nook and corner where a soul can find a false refuge. Be so thorough and discriminating as to render it as nearly impossible as the nature of the case will admit that the inquirer should entertain a false hope.

36th. Do not fear to be thorough. Do not through false pity put on a plaster where the probe is needed. Do not fear that you shall discourage the convicted sinner and turn him back by searching him out to the bottom. If the Holy Spirit is dealing with him, the more you search and probe the more impossible it will be for the soul to turn back or rest in sin.

37th. If you would save the soul, do not spare a right hand or right eye, or any darling idol; but see to it that every form of sin is given up. Insist upon full confession of wrong to all that have a right to confession. Insist upon full restitution, so far as is possible, to all injured parties. Do not fall short of the express teaching of Christ on this subject. Whoever the sinner may be, let him distinctly understand that unless he forsakes all that he has he cannot be the disciple of Christ. Insist upon entire and universal consecration of all the powers of body and mind, and of all the property, possessions, character, and influence to God. Insist upon the total abandonment to God of all ownership of self, or anything else, as a condition of being accepted.

38th. Understand yourself, and, if possible, make the sinner understand, that nothing short of this is involved in true faith or true repentance, and that true consecration involves them all.

39th. Keep constantly before the sinner's mind that it is the *personal* Christ with whom he is dealing, that *God in Christ* is seeking his reconciliation to Himself, and that the condition of his reconciliation is that he gives up his will and his whole being to God — that he "leave not a hoof behind."

40th. Assure him that "God has given to him eternal life, and this life is in His Son"; that "Christ is made unto him wisdom, righteousness, sanctification, and redemption"; and that from first to last he is to find his whole salvation in Christ.

41st. When satisfied that the soul intelligently receives all this doctrine, and the Christ herein revealed, instruct him in the basic precepts of the Christian life. Warn him that sin consists in carnal-mindedness, in "obeying the desires of the flesh and of the mind," and challenge him with the truth that "to be spiritually minded is life and peace."

42nd. Instruct him about the indwelling Holy Spirit, by whose unction and power all victory against Satan comes. And exhort him to "run with patience the race that is set before him, ever looking unto Jesus, the author and finisher of his faith" — that he may "adorn the doctrine of God our Saviour in all things," be "approved in Christ," and ultimately gain the victor's crown.

8

Preacher, Save Thyself

"Take heed unto thyself, and unto the doctrine; continue in them: for in doing this thou shalt both save thyself and them that hear thee" — 1 Tim. 4:16.

I am not going to preach to preachers, but to suggest certain means whereby they may save themselves from sorrow and failure and from the disapproval and reproof of Him who has called them to His service.

1st. See that you are constrained by love to preach the gospel, as Christ was to provide a gospel.

2nd. See that you have the special enduement of power from on high, by the baptism of the Holy Ghost.

3rd. See that you have a heart, and not merely a head call to undertake the preaching of the gospel. By this I mean, be heartily and most intensely inclined to seek the salvation of souls as the great work of life, and do not undertake what you have no heart to.

4th. Constantly maintain a close walk with God.

5th. Make the Bible your book of books. Study it much, upon your knees, waiting for divine light.

6th. Beware of leaning on commentaries. Consult them when convenient; but judge for yourself, in the light of the Holy Spirit.

7th. Keep yourself pure — in will, in thought, in feeling, in word and action.

8th. Contemplate much the guilt and danger of sinners, that your zeal for their salvation may be intensified.

9th. Also deeply ponder and dwell much upon the boundless love and compassion of Christ for them.

10th. So love them yourself as to be willing to die for them.

11th. Give your most intense thought to the study of ways and means by which you may save them. Make this the great and intense study of your life.

12th. Refuse to be diverted from this work. Guard against every temptation that would abate your interest in it.

13th. Believe the assertion of Christ that He is

with you in this work always and everywhere, to give you all the help you need.

14th. "He that winneth souls is wise"; and "If any man lack wisdom, let him ask of God, who giveth to all men liberally and upbraideth not, and he shall receive." "But let him ask in faith." Remember, therefore, that you are bound to have the wisdom that shall win souls to Christ.

15th. Being called of God to the work, make your calling your constant argument with God for all that you need for the accomplishment of the work.

16th. Be diligent and active, "in season and out of season."

17th. Converse much with all classes of your hearers on the question of their salvation, that you may understand their opinions, errors, and needs. Ascertain their prejudices, ignorance, temper, habits, and whatever you need to know to adapt your instruction to their necessities.

18th. See that your own habits are in all respects correct; that you are temperate in all things — free from the stain or smell of tobacco, alcohol, drugs, or anything of which you have reason to be ashamed, and which may stumble others.

19th. Be not "light-minded," but "set the Lord always before you."

20th. Bridle your tongue, and be not given to idle and unprofitable conversation.

21st. Always let your people see that you are

in solemn earnest with them, both in the pulpit and out of it; and let not your daily contacts with them nullify your serious teaching on the Lord's Day.

22nd. Resolve to "know nothing" among your people "save Jesus Christ and Him crucified"; and let them understand that as an ambassador of Christ your business with them relates wholly to the salvation of their souls.

23rd. Be sure to teach them as well by example as by precept. Practise yourself what you preach.

24th. Be especially guarded in your contacts with women, to raise no thought or suspicion of the least impurity in yourself.

25th. Guard your weak points. If naturally tending to gaiety and trifling, watch against occasions for failure in this direction.

26th. If naturally somber and unsocial, guard against moroseness and unsociability.

27th. Avoid all affectation and sham in all things. Be what you profess to be, and you will have no temptation to "make believe."

28th. Let simplicity, sincerity, and Christian propriety stamp your whole life.

29th. Spend much time every day and night in prayer and direct communion with God. This will make you a power for salvation. No amount of learning and study can compensate for the loss of this communion. If you fail to maintain communion with God, you are "weak as another man."

30th. Beware of the error that there are no

means of regeneration, and, consequently, no connection of means and ends in the regeneration of souls.

31st. Understand that conversion is a moral and therefore a voluntary change.

32nd. Understand that the gospel is adapted to change the hearts of men, and in a wise presentation of it you may expect the efficient co-operation of the Holy Spirit.

33rd. In the selection and treatment of your texts, always secure the direct teaching of the Holy Spirit.

34th. Let all your sermons be heart and not merely head sermons.

35th. Preach from experience and not from hearsay, or from mere reading and study.

36th. Always present the subject which the Holy Spirit lays upon your heart for the occasion. Seize the points presented by the Holy Spirit to your own mind, and present them with the greatest possible directness to your congregation.

37th. Be full of prayer whenever you attempt to preach, and go from your closet to your pulpit with the inward groanings of the Spirit pressing for utterance at your lips.

38th. Get your mind fully imbued with your subject, so that it will press for utterance; then open your mouth, and let it forth like a torrent.

39th. See that "the fear of man that bringeth a snare" is not upon you. Let your people understand that you fear God too much to be afraid of them.

40th. Never let the question of your popularity with your people influence your preaching.

41st. Never let the question of salary deter you from "declaring the whole counsel of God, whether men will hear or forbear."

42nd. Do not temporize, lest you lose the confidence of your people and thus fail to save them. They cannot thoroughly respect you, as an ambassador of Christ, if they see that you dare not do your duty.

43rd. Be sure to "commend yourself to every man's conscience in the sight of God."

44th. Be "not a lover of filthy lucre."

45th. Avoid every appearance of vanity.

46th. So live and labor as to compel your people to respect your sincerity and your spiritual wisdom.

47th. Let them not for one moment suppose that you can be influenced in your preaching by any considerations of salary, more or less, or none at all.

48th. Do not make the impression that you are fond of good dinners and like to be invited out to dine; for this will be a snare to you and a stumbling block to them.

49th. Keep your body under, lest after having preached to others, you yourself should be a castaway.

50th. "Watch for souls as one who must give an account to God."

51st. Be a diligent student, and thoroughly instruct your people in all that is essential to their salvation.

52nd. Never flatter the rich.

53rd. Be especially attentive to the needs and the instruction of the poor.

54th. Do not allow yourself to be bribed into a compromise with sin by donation parties.

55th. Do not allow yourself to be publicly treated as a mendicant, or you will be despised by a large class of your hearers.

56th. Repel every attempt to close your mouth against whatever is extravagant, wrong, or injurious among your people.

57th. Maintain your pastoral integrity and independence, lest you sear your conscience, quench the Holy Spirit, forfeit the confidence of your people, and lose the favor of God.

58th. Be an example to the flock, and let your life illustrate your teaching. Remember that your actions and spirit will teach even more impressively than your sermons.

59th. If you preach that men should offer to God and their neighbor a love service, see that you do this yourself, and avoid all that tends to the belief that you are working for pay.

60th. Give to your people a love service, and encourage them to render to you not a money equivalent for your labor but a love reward that will refresh both you and them.

61st. Repel every proposal to get money for

you or for church purposes that will naturally dis-
gust and excite the contempt of worldly but
thoughtful men.

62nd. Resist the introduction of tea parties,
amusing lectures, and dissipating socials, especially at those seasons most favorable for united
efforts to convert souls to Christ. Be sure the devil
will try to head you off in this direction. When you
are praying and planning for a revival of God's
work, some of your worldly church members will
invite you to a party. Go not, or you are in for a
cycle of them, which will defeat your prayers.

63rd. Do not be deceived. Your spiritual power
with your people will never be increased by accepting invitations at such times. If it is a good time to
have parties, because the people have leisure, it is
also a good time for religious meetings, and your
influence should be used to draw the people to the
house of God.

64th. See that you personally know and daily
live upon Christ.

9

Innocent Amusements

We hear much said, and read much in these days, about indulging in innocent amusements. I heard a minister some time ago, in addressing a large company of young people, say that he had spent much time in devising innocent amusements for the young. Within the past few years I have read several sermons and numerous articles pleading for more amusements than have been customary with religious people. With your consent, I wish to suggest a few thoughts upon this subject — first, what are not, and, secondly, what are *innocent* amusements.

1st. This is a question of morals.

2nd. All intelligent acts of a moral agent must be either right or wrong. Nothing is innocent in a moral agent that is not in accordance with the law and gospel of God.

3rd. The moral character of any and every act of a moral agent resides in the motive or the ultimate reason for the act. This I take to be self-evident and universally admitted.

4th. Now, what is the rule of judgment in *this* case? How are we to decide whether any given act of amusement is right or wrong, innocent or sinful?

I answer: 1st. By the moral law, "Thou shalt love the Lord thy God with all thy heart," etc., "and thy neighbor as thyself." No intelligent act of a moral agent is innocent or right unless it proceeds from and is an expression of supreme love to God and equal love to man — in other words, unless it is benevolent. 2nd. By the gospel. This requires the same: "Therefore, whether ye eat or drink, or whatever ye do, do all to the glory of God." "Do all in the name of our Lord Jesus Christ." 3rd. Right reason affirms the same thing.

Now, in the light of this rule, it is plain that it is not innocent to engage in amusements merely to gratify the desire for amusement. We may not innocently eat or drink to gratify the desire for food or drink. To eat or drink to gratify the appetite is innocent enough in a mere animal, but in a moral agent it is a sin. A moral agent is bound to have a higher ultimate motive — to eat and drink that he may be strong and healthy for the service of God. God has made eating and drinking pleasant to us; but this pleasure ought not to be our ultimate reason for eating and drinking. So amusements are pleasant, but this does not justify us in seeking amusements to gratify desire. Mere animals may do this innocently, because they are incapable of any higher motive. But moral agents are under a *higher* law, and are bound to have another and a *higher* aim than merely to gratify the desire for amusements. Therefore, no amusement is innocent which is engaged in for the pleasure of the amusement, any more than it would be innocent to eat and drink for the pleasure of it.

Again, no amusement is innocent that is engaged in merely because we need amusements. We need food and drink; but this does not justify us in eating and drinking simply because we need it. The law of God does not say, "Seek whatever ye need because ye need it"; but, "Do all from love to God and man." A wicked man might eat and drink selfishly — that is, to make his body strong to execute his selfish plans — and this eating and drinking would be *sin* even though he needed food and drink.

Nothing is innocent unless it proceeds from supreme love to God and equal love to man; unless the supreme and ultimate motive be to please and honor God. In other words, to be innocent, any amusement must be engaged in because it is believed to be at the time most pleasing to God and is intended to be a service rendered to Him — a service which, upon the whole, will honor Him more than anything else that we can engage in for the time being. I take this to be self-evident. What then? It follows:

1st. That none but benevolent amusements can be innocent. Fishing and shooting for amusement are not innocent. We may fish and hunt for the same reason that we are allowed to eat and drink — to supply nature with aliment, that we may be strong in the service of God. We may hunt to destroy noxious animals, for the glory of God and the interests of His kingdom. But fishing and hunting to gratify a passion for these sports is not innocent.

Again, no amusement can be innocent that involves the squandering of precious time, that might be better employed to the glory of God and the good of man. Life is short. Time is precious. We have but one life to live. Much is to be done. The world is in darkness. A world of sinners are to be enlightened and, if possible, saved. We are required to work while the day lasts. Our commission and work require dispatch. No time is to be lost. If our hearts are right, our work is pleasant. If rightly performed, it affords the highest enjoyment and is itself the highest amusement. No turning aside for amusement can be innocent that involves any unnecessary loss of time. No man who realizes the greatness of the work to be done, and loves to do it, can turn aside for any amusement involving an unnecessary waste of time.

Again, no amusement can be innocent that

involves an unnecessary expenditure of the Lord's money. All our time and all our money are the Lord's. We are the Lord's. We may innocently use both time and money to promote the Lord's interests and the highest interests of man, which are the Lord's interests. But we may not innocently use either for our own pleasure and gratification. Expensive journeys for our own pleasure and amusement, and not undertaken with a single eye to the glory of God, are not innocent amusements but sinful.

Again, in the light of the above rule of judgment, we see that no form of amusement is lawful for an unconverted sinner. Nothing in him is innocent. While he remains impenitent and unbelieving, does not love God and his neighbor according to God's command, there is for him no innocent employment or amusement; all is sin.

And right here I fear that many are acting under a great delusion. The loose manner in which this subject is viewed by many professing Christians, and even ministers, is surprising and alarming. Some time ago, in a sermon, I remarked that there were no lawful employments or innocent amusements for sinners. An aged clergyman who was present said, after the service, that it was ridiculous to hold that nothing was lawful or innocent in an impenitent sinner. I replied: "I thought you were orthodox. Do you not believe in the universal necessity of regeneration by the Holy Spirit? He replied: "Yes." I added: "Do you believe that an unregenerate soul does anything acceptable to God? Before his heart is changed, does he ever act from a motive that God can accept, in anything whatever? Is he not totally depraved, in the sense that his heart is all wrong, and therefore his actions must be all wrong?" He appeared embarrassed, saw the point, and subsided.

Whatever is lawful in a moral agent or according to the law of God is right. If anyone, therefore, engages lawfully in any employment or in any amusement, he must do so from supreme love to God and equal love to his neighbor; and is, therefore, not an impenitent sinner but a Christian. It is simply absurd and a contradiction to say that an impenitent soul does, or says, or omits anything with a right heart. If impenitent, his ultimate motive must necessarily be wrong; and, consequently, nothing in him is innocent, but all must be sinful. What, then, is an innocent amusement? It must be that and only that which not only might be but actually *is* engaged in with a single eye to God's glory and the interests of His kingdom. If this be not the ultimate and supreme design, it is not an innocent but a sinful amusement. Now, right here is the delusion of many persons, I fear. When speaking of amusements, they say: "What harm is there in them?" In answering to themselves and others this question, they do not penetrate to the bottom of it. If on the surface they see nothing contrary to morality, they judge that the amusement is innocent. They fail to inquire into the supreme and ultimate motive in which the innocence or sinfulness of the act is found. But apart from the motive no course of action is either innocent or sinful, any more than the motions of a machine or the acts of a mere animal are innocent or sinful. No act or course of action should, therefore, be adjudged as either innocent or sinful without ascertaining the supreme motive of the person who acts.

To teach, either directly or by implication, that any amusement of an impenitent sinner or of a backslider is innocent is to teach a gross and ruinous heresy. Parents should remember this in regard to the amusements of their unconverted children. Sunday School teachers and superintendents who are planning amusements for their Sunday Schools, preachers who spend their time in planning amusements for the young, who lead their flocks to picnics, in pleasure excursions, and justify various games, should certainly remember that unless they are in a holy state of heart, and do all this from supreme love to God and a design in the highest degree to glorify God thereby, these ways of spending time are by no means innocent but highly criminal, and those who teach people to walk in these ways are simply directing the channels in which their depravity shall run. For be it ever remembered that unless these things are indulged in from supreme love to God and designed to glorify Him — unless they are, in fact, engaged in with a single eye to the glory of God — they are not innocent but sinful amusements. I must say again, and, if possible, still more emphatically, that it is not enough that they might be engaged in as the best way, for the time being, to honor and please God; but they must be actually engaged in from supreme love to God, with the ultimate design to glorify Him.

If such, then, is the true doctrine of innocent amusements, let no impenitent sinner and no backslidden Christian suppose for a moment that it is possible for him to engage in any innocent amusement. If it were true, as the aged minister to whom I have referred and many others seem to believe, that impenitent sinners or backsliders can and do engage in innocent amusements, the very engaging in such amusements, being lawfully right and innocent in them, would involve a change of heart in the unconverted and a return to God in the backslider. For no amusement is lawful unless it be engaged in as a love-service rendered to God and with design to please and glorify Him. It must not only be a love-service, but, in the judgment of the one who renders it, it must be the best service that, for the time being, he can render to God — a service that will be more pleasing to Him and more useful to His kingdom than any other that can be engaged in at the time. Let these facts be borne in mind when the question of engaging in amusements comes up for decision. And remember, the question in all such cases is not, "What harm is there in this proposed amusement?" but, "What good can it do?" "Is it the best way in which I can spend my time?" "Will it be more pleasing to God and more for the interests of His kingdom than anything else at present possible to me?" If not, it is not an innocent amusement, and I cannot engage in it without sin.

The question often arises: "Are we never to seek such amusements?" I answer: It is our privilege and our duty to live above a desire for such things. All that class of desires should be so subdued by living so much in the light of God and having so deep a communion with Him as not to feel the necessity of worldly excitements, sports, pastimes and entertainments to make his enjoyment satisfactory. If a Christian avails himself of his privilege of communion with God, he will naturally and by an instinct of his new nature repel solicitation to go after worldly amusements. To him such pastimes will appear low, unsatisfactory, and even repulsive. If he is of a heavenly mind, as he ought to be, he will feel as if he could not afford to come down and seek enjoyment in worldly amusements.

Surely a Christian must be fallen from his first love, he must have turned back into the world, before he can feel the necessity or have the desire of seeking enjoyment in worldly sports and pastimes. A spiritual mind cannot seek enjoyment in worldly society. To such a mind that society is necessarily repulsive. Worldly society is insincere, hollow, and to a great extent a sham. What relish can a spiritual mind have for the gossip of a worldly party of pleasure? None whatever. To a mind in communion with God their worldly spirit and ways, conversation and folly is repulsive and painful, as it is so strongly suggestive of the downward tendency of their souls and of the destiny that awaits them.

I have had so marked an experience of both sides of this question that I think I cannot be mistaken. Probably few persons enjoy worldly pleasure more intensely than I did before I was converted; but my conversion, and the spiritual baptism which immediately followed it, completely extinguished all desire for worldly sports and amusements. I was lifted at once into entirely another plane of life and another kind of enjoyment. From that hour to the present the mode of life, the pastimes, sports, amusements, and worldly ways that so much delighted me before have not only failed to interest me, but I have had a positive aversion to them. I have never felt them necessary to, or even compatible with, a truly rational enjoyment. I do not speak boastingly; but for the honor of Christ and His religion I must say that my Christian life has been a happy one. I have found as much enjoyment as is probably best for men to have in one life, and never for an hour have I had the desire to turn back and seek enjoyment from anything the world can give.

But some may ask: "Suppose we do not find sufficient enjoyment in religion, and really desire to go after worldly amusements. If we have the disposition, is it not as well to gratify it?" "Is there any more sin in seeking amusements than in entertaining a longing for them?" I reply that a longing for them should never be entertained. It is the privilege and therefore the duty of everyone to rise, through grace, above a hungering and thirsting for the fleshpots of Egypt, worldly pastimes and time-wasting amusements. The indulgence of such longings is not innocent. One should not ask whether the longing should be gratified, but whether it should not be displaced by a longing for the glory of God and His kingdom.

Professed Christians are bound to maintain a life consistent with their profession. For the honor of religion they ought to deny worldly lusts, and not, by seeking to gratify them, give occasion to the world to scoff and say that Christians love the world as well as *they* do. If professors of Christ are backslidden in heart and entertain a longing for worldly sports and amusements,   they are bound by every consideration of duty and decency to abstain from all outward manifestation of such inward lustings. Some have maintained that we should conform to the ways of the world somewhat — at least enough to show that we can enjoy the world and religion too; and that we make religion appear repulsive to unconverted souls by turning our backs upon what they call their innocent amusements. But we should represent religion as it really is — as living above the world, as consisting in a heavenly mind, as that which affords an enjoyment so spiritual and heavenly as to render the low pursuits and joys of worldly men disagreeable and repulsive. It is a sad stumbling block to the unconverted to see professed Christians seeking pleasure or happiness from this world. Such seeking is a misrepresentation of the religion of Jesus. It misleads, bewilders, and confounds the observing outsider. If he ever reads his Bible, he cannot but wonder that souls who are born of God and have communion with Him should have any relish for worldly ways and pleasures. The fact is that thoughtful unconverted men have little or no confidence in that class of professing Christians who seek enjoyment from this world. They may profess to have, and may loosely think of such as being liberal and good Christians. They may flatter them, and commend their religion as being the opposite of fanaticism and bigotry, and as being such a religion as they like to see; but there is no real sincerity in such professions on the part of the impenitent.

In my early Christian life I heard a Methodist bishop from the South report a case that made a deep impression on my mind. He said there was in his neighborhood a slaveholder, a gentleman of fortune, who was a jovial and agreeable man and gave himself much to various field sports and amusements. He used to associate much with his pastor, often inviting him to dinner and to accompany him in his sports and pleasure-seeking excursions of various kinds. The minister cheerfully complied with these requests and a friendship grew up between the pastor and his parishioner that continued till the last sickness of this jovial and wealthy man. When the wife of this worldling was apprised that her husband could live but a short time, she was much alarmed for his soul and tenderly inquired if she should not call in their minister to converse and pray with him. He feelingly replied: "No, my dear. He is not the man for me to see now. He was my companion, as you know, in worldly sports and pleasure-seeking; he loved good dinners and a jolly time. I then enjoyed his society and found him a pleasant companion. But I see now that I never had any confidence in his piety, and have now no confidence in the efficacy of his prayers. I am now a dying man, and need the instruction and prayers of somebody who can prevail with God. We have been much together, but our pastor has never been in earnest with me about the salvation of my soul, and he is not the man to help me now." The wife was greatly affected, and said: "What shall I do, then?" He replied: "My coachman, Tom, is a pious man. I have confidence in his prayers. I have often overheard him pray, when about the barn or stables, and his prayers have always struck me as being quite sincere and earnest. I never heard any foolishness from him. He has always been honest and earnest as a Christian man. Call him." Tom was called, and came within the door, dropping his hat and looking tenderly and compassionately at his dying master. The dying man put forth his hand, saying: "Come here, Tom. Take my hand. Tom, can you pray for your dying master?" Tom poured out his soul in earnest prayer.

I cannot remember the name of this bishop, it was so long ago; but the story I well remember as an illustration of the mistake into which many professing Christians and some ministers fall, supposing that we recommend religion to the unconverted by mingling with them in their pleasures and their running after amusements. I have seen many illustrations of this mistake. Christians should live so far above the world as not to need or seek its pleasures, and thus recommend religion to the world as a source of the highest and purest happiness. The peaceful look, the joyful countenance, the spiritual serenity and cheerfulness of a living Christian recommend religion to the unconverted. Their satisfaction in God, their holy joy, their living above and shunning the ways and amusements of worldly minds impress the unconverted with a sense of the necessity and desirableness of a Christian life. But let no man think he will gain a really Christian influence over another by manifesting a sympathy with his worldly aspirations.

Now, is this rule a yoke of bondage? I do not wonder that it has created in some minds not a little disturbance. The pleasure-loving and pleasure-seeking members of the Church regard the rule as impracticable, as a strait jacket, as a bondage. But to whom is it a strait jacket and a bondage? To whom is it impracticable? Surely it is not and cannot be to any who love God with all their heart and their neighbor as themselves. It certainly cannot be so regarded by a real Christian, for all real Christians love God supremely. Their own interests and their own pleasure are regarded as nothing as compared with the interests and good pleasure of God. They, therefore, cannot seek amusements unless they believe themselves called of God to do so. By a law of our nature we seek to please those whom we supremely love. Also, by a law of our nature we find our highest *happiness* in pleasing those whom we supremely love; and we supremely please ourselves when we seek not at all to please ourselves but to please the object of our supreme affection. Therefore, Christians find their highest enjoyment and their truest pleasure in pleasing God and in seeking the good of their fellow-men; and they enjoy this service all the more because enjoyment is not what they *seek* but what they inevitably experience by a law of their nature.

This is a fact of Christian consciousness. The highest and purest of all amusements is found in doing the will of God. Mere worldly amusements are cold and insipid and not worthy of naming in comparison with the enjoyment we find in doing the will of God. To one who loves God supremely it is natural to seek amusements, and everything else that we seek, with supreme reference to the glory of God. Why, then, should this rule be regarded as too strict, as placing the standard too high, and as being a strait jacket and a bondage? How, then, are we to understand those who plead so much for worldly amusements?

From what I have heard and read upon this subject within the last few years, I have gathered that these pleaders for amusements have thought that there was more enjoyment to be gained from these amusements than from the service of God. They remind me of a sentence that I used to have to copy when a schoolboy: "All work and no play makes Jack a dull boy." They seem to assume that the service of God is work in the sense of being a task and a burden; that to labor and pray and preach to win souls to Christ, to commune with God and perform the duties of religion is so wearisome, not to say irksome, that we need a good many playdays; that the love of Christ is not satisfactory; that we must have frequent resort to worldly amusements to make life tolerable. Christ on one occasion said to His disciples: "Come aside and rest a while." This is not surprising when we consider that they were often so thronged as not to have time even to eat their ordinary meals. But it was not amusement that they sought — simply rest from their labors of love, in which labors they must have had the greatest enjoyment.

I often ask myself: "What can it mean that so many of our highly fed and most popular preachers are pleading so much for amusements?" They seem to be leading the Church off in a direction in which she is the most in danger. It is no wonder that lay men and women are easily led in that direction, for such teaching exactly accords with the innumerable temptations to worldliness which are presented to the Church on every side. The Bible is replete with instruction upon this subject, which is the direct opposite of these pleas for worldly amusements. These teachers plead for fun, hilarity, jesting, plays, games, and such things as worldly minds love and enjoy; but the Bible exhorts to sobriety, heavenly-mindedness, unceasing prayer, and a close and perpetual walk with God. The Bible everywhere assumes that all real enjoyment is found in this course of life, that all true peace of mind is found in communion with God and in being given up to seek His glory as the constant and supreme end of life. It exhorts us to watchfulness, and informs us that for every idle word we must give account in the Day of Judgment. It nowhere informs us that fun and hilarity are the source of rational enjoyment; it nowhere encourages us to expect or maintain a close walk with God, to have peace of mind and joy in the Holy Ghost, if we gad about to seek amusements. And is not the teaching of the Bible on this subject in exact accordance with human experience? Do we need to have the pulpit turn advocate of worldly amusements? Is not human depravity strong enough in that direction, without being stimulated by the voice of the preacher? Has the Church worked so hard for God and souls, are Christians so overdone

with their exhausting efforts to pull sinners out of
the fire, that they are in danger of becoming insane
with religious fervor and need that the pulpit and
the press should join in urging them to turn aside
and seek amusements and have a little fun? What
can it mean? Why, is it not true that nearly all our
dangers are on this side? Is not human nature in its
present state so strongly tending in these directions
that we need to be on our guard, and constantly to
exhort the Church *not* to be led away after amusements and fun, to the destruction of their souls?
But to come back to the question: To whom is it a
bondage to be required to have a single eye to the
good pleasure and glory of God in all that we do?
Who finds it hard to do so? Christ says His yoke is
easy and His burden is light. The requirement to do
all for the glory of God is surely none other than
the yoke of Christ. It is His expressed will. Who
finds this a hard yoke and a heavy burden? It is not
hard or heavy to a willing, loving mind.

   Just the thing here required is natural and inevitable to everyone who truly loves God and is truly
devoted to the Saviour. What is devotion to Jesus
but a heart set upon rendering Him a loving obedience in all things? What is Christian liberty but
the privilege of doing that which Christians most
love to do — that is, in all things to fulfill the good
pleasure of their blessed Lord? Turn aside from
saving souls to seek amusements! As if there could
be a higher and diviner pleasure than is found in
laboring for the salvation of souls. It cannot be.

There can be no higher enjoyment found in this world than is found in pulling souls out of the fire and bringing them to Christ. I am filled with amazement when I read and hear the appeals to the Church to seek more worldly amusements. Do we need, can we have any fuller and higher satisfaction than is found in a close, serious, loving walk with God and co-operation with Him in fitting souls for heaven?

All that I hear said to encourage the people of God in seeking amusements appears to me to proceed from a worldly instead of a spiritual state of mind. Can it be possible that a soul in communion with God and, of course, yearning with compassion over dying men, struggling from day to day in agonizing prayer for their salvation, should entertain the thought of turning aside to seek amusement? Can a pastor in whose congregation are numbers of unsaved souls, and among whose membership are many worldly-minded professing Christians, turn aside and lead or accompany his church in a backsliding movement to gain worldly pleasure? There are always enough in every church who are easily led astray in that direction. But who are they that most readily fall in with such a movement? Who are ready to come to the front when a picnic, a pleasure excursion, a worldly party, or other pleasure-seeking activities are proposed? Are they, in fact, the class that always attend prayer meetings, that are always in a revival state of mind? Do they belong to the class whose faces shine from day to day with the peace of God pervading their souls? Are they the Aarons and Hurs that stay up the hands of their pastor with continual and prevailing prayer? Are they spiritual members, whose conversation is in heaven and who mind not earthly things? Who does not know that it is the worldly members in the congregation who are always ready for any movement in the direction of worldly pleasure or amusement, and that the truly spiritual, prayerful, heavenly-minded members are shy of all such movements? They are not led into them without urging, and weep in secret places when they see their pastor giving encouragement to that which is likely to be so great a stumbling block to both the Church and to the world.

————

President Finney of Oberlin College, in forwarding his revision of the above tract for publication by the Willard Tract Repository, accompanied it with a note to Dr. Cullis, in which he said:

"The previous pages contain a condensation of three short articles that I published in the *Independent*. I recollect that the editor of the *Advance,* and one of the editors of the *Independent* — both of whom had published what I regard as very loose views, approving and recommending the worldly amusements of Christians — criticized those articles with an asperity that seemed to indicate that they were nettled by them. They so far perverted them as to assert that they taught asceticism, and the prohibition of *rest,* recreation, and *all* amusements. I regard the doctrine of this tract as strictly Biblical and true. But, to avoid all such unjust inferences and cavils, add the following lines.

"Let no one say that the doctrine of this tract prohibits all rest, recreation, and amusement whatever. It does not. It freely allows for all rest, recreation, and amusement that is regarded, by the person who resorts to it, as a condition and *means* of securing health and vigor of body and mind with which to promote the cause of God. This tract only insists, as the Bible does, that 'whether we eat or drink,' rest, recreate, or amuse ourselves, all must be done as a service rendered to God. God must be our end. To please Him must be our aim in everything, or we sin."

10

How to Overcome Sin

In every period of my ministerial life I have found many professed Christians in a miserable state of bondage, either to the world, the flesh, or the devil. But surely this is no Christian state, for the apostle has distinctly said: "Sin shall not have dominion over you, because ye are not under the law, but under grace." In all my Christian life I have been pained to find so many Christians living in the legal bondage described in the seventh chapter of Romans — a life of sinning, resolving to reform, and falling again. And what is particularly saddening, and even agonizing, is that many ministers and leading Christians give perfectly false instruction upon the subject of how to overcome sin. The directions that are generally given on this subject, I am sorry to say, amount to this: "Take your sins in detail, resolve to abstain from them, and fight against them, if need be with prayer and fasting, until you have overcome them. Set your will *firmly* against a relapse into sin, pray and struggle, and resolve that you will not fall — and persist in this until you form the habit of obedience and break up all your sinful habits." To be sure it is generally added: "In this conflict you must not depend upon your own strength but pray for the help of God." In a word, much of the teaching, both of the pulpit and the Christian press, really amounts to this: Sanctification is by works and not by faith.

I notice that Dr. Chalmers, in his lectures on Romans, expressly maintains that justification is by faith but sanctification is by works. Some twenty-five years ago, I think, a prominent professor of theology in New England maintained in substance the same doctrine. In my early Christian life I was very nearly misled by one of President Edwards's resolutions, which was, in substance, that when he had fallen into any sin he would trace it back to its source, and then fight and pray against it with all his might until he subdued it. This, it will be perceived, is directing the attention to the overt act of sin, its source or occasions. Resolving and fighting against it fastens the attention on the sin and its source, and diverts it entirely from Christ.

Now it is important to say right here that all

such efforts are worse than useless, and not infrequently result in delusion. First, it is losing sight of what really constitutes sin; and, second, it is overlooking the only practicable way to avoid it. In this way the outward act or habit may be overcome and avoided but that which really constitutes the sin is left untouched. Sin is not external but internal. It is not a muscular act, it is not the volition that causes the muscular action, it is not an involuntary feeling or desire; it must be a voluntary act or state of mind. Sin is nothing else than that voluntary, ultimate preference or state of committal to self-pleasing out of which the volitions, the outward actions, purposes, intentions, and all the things that are commonly called sin proceed.

Now, what is resolved against in this religion of resolutions and efforts to suppress sinful and form holy habits? "Love is the fulfilling of the law." But do we produce love by resolution? Do we eradicate selfishness by resolution? No, indeed. We may suppress this or that expression or manifestation of selfishness by resolving not to do this or that, and praying and struggling against it. We may resolve upon an outward obedience, and work ourselves up to the letter of an obedience to God's commandments. But to eradicate selfishness from the breast by resolution is an absurdity. So the effort to obey the commandments of God in spirit — in other words, to attempt to love as the law of God requires by force of resolution — is an absurdity.

There are many who maintain that sin consists in the desires. Be it so. Do we control our desires by force of resolution? We may abstain from the *gratification* of a particular desire by the force of resolution. We may go further, and abstain from the gratification of desire generally in the outward life. But this is not to secure the love of God, which constitutes obedience. Should we become anchorites, immure ourselves in a cell, and crucify all our desires and appetites so far as their indulgence is concerned, we have only avoided certain forms of sin; but the root that really constitutes sin is not touched. Our resolution has not secured love, which is the only real obedience to God. All our battling with sin in the outward life, by the force of resolution, only ends in making us whited sepulchres. All our battling with desire by the force of resolution is of no avail; for in all this, however successful the effort to suppress sin may be in the outward life or in the inward desire, it will only end in delusion, for by force of resolution we cannot love.

All such efforts to overcome sin are utterly futile, and as unscriptural as they are futile. The Bible expressly teaches us that sin is overcome by faith in Christ. "He is made unto us wisdom, righteousness, sanctification, and redemption." "He is the way, the truth, and the life." Christians are said to "purify their hearts by faith" (Acts 15:9). And in Acts 26:18 it is affirmed that the saints are sanctified by faith in Christ. In Romans 9:31, 32 it is affirmed that the Jews attained not to righteousness "because they sought it not by faith, but as it were by the works of the law." The doctrine of the Bible is that Christ saves His people from sin through faith; that Christ's Spirit is received by faith to dwell in the heart. It is faith that works by love. Love is wrought and sustained by faith. By faith Christians "overcome the world, the flesh, and the devil." It is by faith that they "quench the fiery darts of the wicked one." It is by faith that they "put on the Lord Jesus Christ, and put off the old man, with his deeds." It is by faith that we fight "the good fight," and not by resolution. It is by faith that we "stand"; by resolution we fall. "This is the victory that overcometh the world, even our faith." It is by faith that the flesh is kept under and carnal desires subdued. The fact is that it is simply by faith that we receive the Spirit of Christ to work in us, to will and to do according to His good pleasure. He sheds abroad His own love in our hearts, and thereby enkindles ours. Every victory over sin is by faith in Christ; and whenever the mind is diverted from Christ, by resolving and fighting against sin, whether we are aware of it or not, we are acting in our own strength, rejecting the help of Christ, and are under a specious delusion. Nothing but the life and energy of the Spirit of Christ within us can save us from sin, and trust is the uniform and universal condition of the working of this saving energy within us.

How long shall this fact be at least practically

overlooked by the teachers of religion? How deeply rooted in the heart of man is self-righteousness and self-dependence? So deeply that one of the hardest lessons for the human heart to learn is to renounce self-dependence and trust wholly in Christ. When we open the door by implicit trust He enters in and takes up His abode with us and in us. By shedding abroad His love He quickens our whole souls into sympathy with Himself, and in this way, and in this way alone, He purifies our hearts through faith. He sustains our will in the attitude of devotion. He quickens and regulates our affections, desires, appetites and passions, and becomes our sanctification. Very much of the teaching that we hear in prayer and conference meetings, from the pulpit and the press, is so misleading as to render the hearing or reading of such instruction almost too painful to be endured. Such instruction is calculated to beget delusion, discouragement, and a practical rejection of Christ as He is presented in the gospel.

Alas for the blindness that "leads to bewilder" the soul that is longing after deliverance from the power of sin! I have sometimes listened to legal teaching upon this subject until I felt as if I should scream. It is astonishing sometimes to hear Christian men object to the teaching which I have here inculcated — that it leaves us in a passive state, to be saved without our own activity. What darkness is involved in this objection! The Bible teaches that by trusting in Christ we receive an inward influence that stimulates and directs our activity; that by faith we receive His purifying influence into the very center of our being; that through and by His truth revealed directly to the soul He quickens our whole inward being into the attitude of a loving obedience; and this is the way, and the only practicable way, to overcome sin.

But someone may say: "Does not the apostle exhort as follows: 'Work out your own salvation with fear and trembling; for it is God which worketh in you, both to will and to do of His good pleasure'? And is not this an exhortation to do what in this article you condemn?" By no means. In the 12th verse of the second chapter of Philippians Paul says: "Wherefore, my beloved, as ye have always obeyed, not as in my presence only, but now much more in my absence, work out your own salvation with fear and trembling, for it is God that worketh in you, both to will and to do of His good pleasure." There is no exhortation to work by force of resolution, but through and by the inworking of God. Paul had taught them, while he was present with them; but now, in his absence, he exhorts them to work out their own salvation, not by resolution but by the inward operation of God. This is precisely the doctrine of this tract. Paul had too often taught the Church that Christ in the heart is our sanctification, and that this influence is to be received by faith, to be guilty in this passage of teaching that our sanctification is to be wrought out by resolution and efforts to suppress sinful and form holy habits. This passage of Scripture happily recognizes both the divine and human agency in the work of sanctification. God works in us to will and to do; and we, accepting by faith His inworking, will and do according to His good pleasure. Faith itself is an *active* and not a passive state. A passive holiness is impossible and absurd. Let no one say that when we exhort people to trust wholly in Christ we teach that anyone should be or can be passive in receiving and co-operating with the divine influence within. This influence is *moral,* and not physical. It is persuasion, and not force. It influences the free will, and consequently does this by *truth,* and not by force. Oh that it could be understood that the whole of spiritual life that is in *any* man is received direct from the Spirit of Christ by faith, as the branch receives its life from the vine! Away with this religion of resolutions! It is a snare of death. Away with this effort to make the life holy while the heart has not in it the love of God! Oh that we would learn to look directly at Christ through the gospel, and so embrace Him by an act of loving trust as to involve a universal sympathy with His state of mind. This, and this alone, is sanctification.

11

The Decay of Conscience

I believe it is a fact generally admitted that there is much less conscience manifested by men and women in nearly all the walks of life than there was forty years ago. There is justly much complaint of this, and there seems to be but little prospect of reformation. The rings and frauds and villainies in high and low places, among all ranks of men, are most alarming, and one is almost compelled to ask: "Can nobody be safely trusted?" Now, what is the cause of this degeneracy? Doubtless there are many causes that contribute more or less directly to it, but I am persuaded that the fault is more in the ministry and the public press than in any and all things else.

It has been fashionable now for many years to

ridicule and decry Puritanism. Ministers have ceased, in a great measure, to probe the consciences of men with the spiritual law of God. So far as my knowledge extends, there has been a great letting down, an ignoring of the searching claims of God's law as revealed in His Word. This law is the only standard of true morality. "By the law is the knowledge of sin." The law is the quickener of the human conscience. Just in proportion as the spirituality of the law of God is kept out of view will there be manifest a decay of conscience. This must be the inevitable result. Let ministers ridicule Puritanism, attempt to preach the gospel without thoroughly probing the conscience with the divine law, and this *must* result in, at least, a partial paralysis of the moral sense.

The error that lies at the foundation of this decay of individual and public conscience originates, no doubt, in the pulpit. The proper guardians of the public conscience have, I fear, very much neglected to expound and insist upon obedience to the moral law. It is plain that some of our most popular preachers are phrenologists. Phrenology has no organ of free will. Hence, it has no moral agency, no moral law and moral obligation in any proper sense of these terms. A consistent phrenologist can have no proper ideas of moral obligation, of moral guilt, blameworthiness or retribution. Some years ago a brother of one of our most popular preachers heard me preach on the text "Be ye reconciled to God." I went on to show, among other things, that being reconciled to God implied being reconciled to the execution of His law. He called on me the next morning and among other things said that neither himself nor two of his brothers, whom he named — all preachers — had naturally any conscience. "We have," said he, "no such ideas in our minds of sin, guilt, justice and retribution as you and Father have. . . . We cannot preach as you do on those subjects." He continued: "I am striving to cultivate a conscience, and I think I begin to understand what it is. But naturally, neither I nor the two brothers I have named have any conscience."

Now these three ministers have repeatedly appeared in their writings before the public. I have read much that they have written, and not infrequently the sermons of one of them. I have been struck with the manifest lack of conscience in his sermons and writings. He is a phrenologist, and, hence, he has in his theological views no free will, no moral agency, and nothing that is really a logical result of free will and moral agency. He can ridicule Puritanism and the great doctrines of the orthodox faith; and, indeed, his whole teaching, so far as it has fallen under my eye, most lamentably shows the lack of moral discrimination. I should judge from his writings that the true ideas of moral depravity, guilt, and deserved punishment, in the true acceptation of those terms, have no place in his mind. Indeed, as a consistent phrenologist, such ideas have no right in his mind. They are necessarily excluded by his philosophy.

I do not know how extensively phrenology has poisoned the minds of ministers of different denominations, but I have observed with pain that many ministers who write for the public press fail to reach the consciences of men. They fail to go to the bottom of the matter and insist upon obedience to the moral law as alone acceptable to God. They seem to me to "make void the law through faith." They seem to hold up a different standard from that which is inculcated in Christ's Sermon on the Mount, which was Christ's exposition of the moral law. Christ expressly taught in that sermon that there was no salvation without conformity to the rule of life laid down in that sermon. True faith in Christ will always and inevitably beget a holy life. But I fear it has become fashionable to preach what amounts to an antinomian gospel. The rule of life proclaimed in the Gospels is precisely that of the moral law. These four things are expressly affimed of true faith — of the faith of the New Testament.

1st. "It establishes the law."

2nd. "It works by love."

3rd. "It purifies the heart."

4th. "It overcomes the world."

These are but different forms of affirming that true faith does, as a matter of fact, produce a holy life. If it did not, it would "make *void* the law." The true gospel is not preached where obedience to the moral law as the only rule of life is not insisted upon. Wherever there is a failure to do this in the instructions of any pulpit, it will inevitably be seen that the hearers of such a mutilated gospel will have very little conscience. We need more Boanerges or "sons of thunder" in the pulpit. We need men who will flash forth the law of God like livid lightning and arouse the consciences of men. We need more Puritanism in the pulpit. To be sure, some of the Puritans were extremists. But still under their teaching there was a very different state of the individual and public conscience from what exists in these days. Those old, stern, grand vindicators of the government of God would have thundered and lightninged until they had almost demolished their pulpits if any such immoralities had shown themselves under their instructions as are common in these days.

In a great measure the periodical press takes its tone from the pulpit. The universal literature of the present day shows conclusively that the moral sense of the people needs toning up, and some of our most fascinating preachers have become the favorites of infidels, skeptics of every grade, Universalists, and the most abandoned characters. And has the offence of the cross ceased, or is the cross kept out of view? Has the holy law of God, with its stringent precepts and its awful penalty, become popular with unconverted men and women? Or is it ignored in the pulpit and the preacher praised for that neglect of duty for which he should be despised? I believe the only possible way to arrest this downward tendency in private and pub-

lic morals is the holding up from the pulpits in this
land, with unsparing faithfulness, the whole gospel
of God, including as the only rule of life the perfect
and holy law of God.

The holding up of this law will reveal the moral
depravity of the heart, and the holding forth of the
cleansing blood of Christ will cleanse the heart
from sin. My beloved brethren in the ministry, is
there not a great deficiency in the public inculcations of the pulpit upon this subject? We are set for
the defence of the blessed gospel and for the vindi-
cation of God's holy law. I implore you, let us
probe the consciences of our hearers, let us thunder
forth the law and gospel of God until our voices
reach the capital of this nation, through our repre-
sentatives in Congress. It is now very common for
the secular papers even to publish extracts of sermons. Let us give the reporters of the press such
work to do as will make their ears and the ears of
their readers tingle. Let our railroad magnates, our
stock gamblers, our officials of every grade, hear
from its widespread pulpit, if they come within the
sound, such wholesome Puritanic preaching as will
arouse them to better thoughts and a better life.
Away with this milk-and-water preaching of a love
of Christ that has no holiness or moral discrimination in it. Away with preaching a love of God that
is not angry with sinners every day. Away with
preaching a Christ not crucified for sin.

Christ crucified for the sins of the world is the
Christ that the people need. Let us rid ourselves of

the just imputation of neglecting to preach the law of God until the consciences of men are asleep. Such a collapse of conscience in this land could never have existed if the Puritan element in our preaching had not in great measure fallen out.

Some years ago I was preaching in a congregation whose pastor had died some months before. He seemed to have been almost universally popular with his church and the community. His church seemed to have nearly idolized him. Everybody was speaking in his praise and holding him up as an example; and yet both the church and the community clearly demonstrated that they had had an unfaithful minister, a man who loved and sought the applause of his people. I heard so much of his inculcations and saw so much of the legitimate fruits of his teachings that I felt constrained to tell the people from the pulpit that they had had an unfaithful minister; that such fruits as were apparent on every side, both within and without that church, could never have resulted from a faithful presentation of the gospel. This assertion would, doubtless, have greatly shocked them had it been made under other circumstances; but, as the way had been prepared, they did not seem disposed to gainsay it. Brethren, our preaching will bear its legitimate fruits. If immorality prevails in the land, the fault is ours in a great degree. If there is a decay of conscience, the pulpit is responsible for it. If the public press lacks moral discrimination, the pulpit is responsible for it. If the church is degenerate and worldly, the pulpit is responsible for it. If the world loses its interest in religion, the pulpit is responsible for it. If Satan rules in our halls of legislation, the pulpit is responsible for it. If our politics become so corrupt that the very foundations of our government are ready to fall away, the pulpit is responsible for it. Let us not ignore this fact, my dear brethren, but let us lay it to heart, and be thoroughly awake to our responsibility in respect to the morals of this nation.

12

The Psychology of Faith

I have heretofore endeavored to show that sanctification is wrought in the soul by the Spirit of Christ, through faith, with and not without the concurrence of our own activity. I now wish to call attention to the nature or psychology of faith as a mental act or state. My theological teacher held that faith was an intellectual act or state, a conviction or firm persuasion that the doctrines of the Bible are true. So far as I can recollect, this was the view of faith which I heard everywhere advanced.

When it was objected to this that the intellectual convictions and states are involuntary and so cannot be produced by any effort of the will; that, consequently, we could not be under any obligations to exercise faith; and, furthermore, that faith, if an intellectual act or state, could not be a virtue — it was replied that we control the attention of the mind by an effort of the will and that our responsibility therefore lies in searching for that degree of evidence that will convince the intellect; that unbelief is a sin because it is the inevitable result of a failure to search for and accept the evidence of the truths of revelation; and that faith is a virtue because it involves the consent and effort of the will to search out the truth.

I have met with this erroneous notion of the nature of Christian faith often since I was first licensed to preach. Especially in my early ministry I found that great stress was laid on believing "the articles of faith," and it was held that faith consisted in believing with an unwavering conviction the doctrines about Christ. Hence, an acceptance of the doctrines, the *doctrines*, the DOCTRINES of the gospel was very much insisted upon as constituting faith. But these doctrines I had been brought to accept intellectually and firmly before I was converted. And, when told to believe, I replied that I did believe — and no argument or assertion could convince me that I did not believe the gospel. And up to the very moment of my conversion I was not and could not be convinced of my error.

At the moment of my conversion, or when I first exercised faith, I saw my ruinous error. I found that faith consisted not in an intellectual conviction that the things affirmed in the Bible about Christ are true, but in *the heart's trust in the person of Christ.* I learned that God's testimony concerning Christ was designed to lead me to trust Christ, to confide in His person as my Saviour, and that to stop short in merely believing about Christ was a fatal mistake that inevitably left me in my sins. It was as if I were sick almost unto death and someone should recommend to me a physician who was surely able and willing to save my life, and I should listen to the testimony concerning him until fully convinced that he was both able and willing to save my life, and then should be told to believe in him and my life was secure. Now, if I understood this to mean nothing more than to accept the testimony with the firmest conviction, I should reply: "I do believe in him with an undoubting faith. I believe every word you have told me regarding him." But if I stopped here I should, of course, lose my life. In addition to this firm intellectual conviction of his willingness and ability it would be essential to apply to him, to come to him, to trust his person, to accept his treatment. When I had intellectually accepted the testimony concerning him with an unwavering belief, the next and the indispensable thing would be a voluntary act of trust or confidence in his person, a committal of my life to him and his sovereign treatment in the cure of my disease.

Now this illustrates the true nature or psychology of faith as it actually exists in consciousness. It does not consist in any degree of intellectual knowledge or acceptance of the doctrines of the

Bible. The firmest possible persuasion that every word said in the Bible respecting God and Christ is true, is not faith. These truths and doctrines reveal God in Christ only so far as they point to God in Christ and teach the soul how to find Him by an act of trust in His person.

When we firmly trust in His person and commit our souls to Him by an unwavering act of confidence in Him for all that He is affirmed to be to us in the Bible, this is faith. We trust Him upon the testimony of God. We trust Him for what the doctrines and facts of the Bible declare Him to be to us. This act of trust unites our spirit to Him in a union so close that we directly receive from Him a current of eternal life. Faith, in consciousness, seems to complete the divine galvanic circle, and the life of God is instantly imparted to our souls. God's life and light and love and peace and joy seem to flow to us as naturally and spontaneously as the galvanic current from the battery. We then for the first time understand what Christ meant by our being united to Him by faith, as the branch is united to the vine. Christ is then and thus revealed to us as God. We are conscious of direct communion with Him, and know Him as we know ourselves by His direct activity within us. We then know directly, in consciousness, that He is our life, and that we receive from Him, moment by moment, as it were, an impartation of eternal life.

With some the mind is comparatively dark, and the faith, therefore, comparatively weak in its first exercise. They may hold a great breadth of opinion, and yet intellectually believe but little with clear conviction. Hence, their trust in Him will be as narrow as their convictions. When faith is weak, the current of the divine life will flow so mildly that we are scarcely conscious of it. But when faith is strong and all-embracing, it lets a current of the divine life of love into our souls so strong that it seems to permeate both soul and body. We then know in consciousness what it is to have Christ's Spirit within us as a power to save us from sin and keep our feet in the path of loving obedience.

From personal conversation with hundreds — and I may say thousands — of Christian people, I have been struck with the application of Christ's words, as recorded in the fifth chapter of John, to their experience. Christ said to the Jews: "Ye do search the Scriptures [for so it should be rendered], for in them ye think ye have eternal life, and they are they which testify of Me; and ye will not come unto Me that ye might have life." They stopped short in the Scriptures. They satisfied themselves with ascertaining what the Scriptures said *about* Christ but did not avail themselves of the light thus received to come to Him by an act of loving trust in His person. I fear it is true in these days, as it has been in the days that are past, that multitudes stop short in the facts and doctrines of the Bible and do not by any act of trust in Christ's person come to Him, concerning whom all this testimony is given. Thus the Bible is misunderstood and abused.

Many, understanding the "Confession of Faith" as summarizing the doctrines of the Bible, very much neglect the Bible and rest in a belief of the articles of faith. Others, more cautious and more in earnest, search the Scriptures to see what they say about Christ, but stop short and rest in the formation of correct theological opinions. But others, and they are the only saved class, love the Scriptures intensely because they testify of Jesus. They search and devour the Scriptures because they tell them who Jesus is and what they may trust Him for. They do not stop short and rest in this testimony, but by an act of loving trust go directly to Him — to His person — thus joining their souls to Him in a union that receives from Him, by a direct divine communication, the things for which they are led to trust Him. This is certainly Christian experience. This is receiving from Christ the eternal life which God has given us in Him. This is saving faith.

There are many degrees in the strength of faith — from that of which we are hardly conscious to that which lets such a flood of eternal life into the soul as to quite overcome the strength of the body. In the strongest exercise of faith the nerves of the body seem to give way for the time being under the overwhelming exercise of the mind. This great strength of mental exercise is perhaps not very common. We can endure but little of God's light and love in our souls and yet remain in the body. I have sometimes felt that a little clearer vision would draw my soul entirely away from the body, and I have met with many Christian people to whom these strong gales of spiritual influence were familiar. But my object in writing thus is to illustrate the nature or psychology and results of saving faith.

The contemplation of the attitude and experience of numbers of professed Christians in regard to Christ brings surprise and disappointment, considering that the Bible is in their hands. Many of them appear to have stopped short in theological *opinions* more or less firmly held. This they understand to be faith. Others are more in earnest, and stop not short of a more or less certain *conviction* of the truths of the Bible concerning Christ. Others have strong impressions of the obligations of the law, which move them to begin an earnest life of works — which leads them into bondage. They pray from a sense of duty; they are dutiful, but not loving, not confiding. They have no peace and no rest, except in cases where they persuade themselves that they have done their duty. They are in a restless, agonizing state.

> "Reason they hear, her counsels weigh,
>   And all her words approve,
>   And yet they find it hard to obey,
>   And harder still to love."

They read and perhaps search the Scriptures to learn their duty and to learn about Christ. They intellectually believe all that they understand the Scriptures to say about Him. But when Christ is thus commended to their confidence, they do not by an act of personal committal to Him so join their souls to Him as to receive from Him the influx of His life and light and love. They do not by a simple act of personal loving trust in His person receive the current of His divine life and power into their own souls. They do not thus take hold of His strength and interlock their being with His. In other words, they do not truly believe. Hence, they are not saved. Oh, what a mistake is this! I fear it is very common. No, it seems to be certain that it is appallingly common, else how can the state of the Church be accounted for? Is that which we see in the great mass of church members *all* that Christ does for and in His people when they truly believe? No, no! There is great error here. The psychology of faith is mistaken, and an intellectual conviction of the truth of the gospel is supposed to be faith. And some whose opinions seem to be right in regard to the nature of faith rest in their philosophy and fall short of *exercising* faith.

Let no one suppose that I underestimate the value of the facts and doctrines of the Bible. I regard a knowledge and belief of them as of fundamental importance. I have no sympathy with those who undervalue them and treat doctrinal discussion and preaching as of minor importance, nor can I assent to the teaching of those who would have us preach Christ and not the doctrines respecting Him. It is the facts and doctrines of the Bible that teach us who Christ is, why He is to be trusted, and for what. How can we preach Christ without preaching about Him? And how can we trust Him without being informed why and for what we are to trust Him?

The error to which I call attention does not consist in laying too much stress on teaching and believing the facts and doctrines of the Word; but it consists in stopping short of trusting the personal Christ for what those facts and doctrines teach us to trust Him, and satisfying ourselves with believing the testimony concerning Him — thus resting in the belief of what God has said about Him instead of committing our souls to Him by an act of loving trust.

The testimony of God respecting Him is designed to secure our confidence in Him. If it fails to secure the uniting of our souls to Him by an act of implicit trust in Him — such an act of trust as unites us to Him as the branch is united to the vine — we have heard the gospel in vain. We are not saved. We have failed to receive from Him that impartation of eternal life which can be conveyed to us through no other channel than that of implicit trust.

13

The Psychology of Righteousness

During my Christian life I have been asked a great many times, in substance, by thoughtful and anxious souls: "What is the mental act and state (or the acts and states) that God requires of me?" I have found it profitable, even indispensable, with the commands of God before me, to question my consciousness for a satisfactory answer to this question. I have satisfied myself, and, by the help of God, I trust I have aided many others to their satisfaction. Be it understood, then, that by "the psychology of righteousness" I mean the mental act and state that constitutes righteousness. I will endeavor to develop this theme in the following order by showing:

I. What righteousness is not.

II. What it is.

III. How we know what righteousness is.

IV. How a sinner may attain to righteousness.

I. What righteousness is not.

1. Righteousness does not consist of anything in the outward life or in any physical or bodily act whatever. All such acts belong to the category of cause and effect. They are necessitated by an act of the will and have in themselves no moral character whatever.

2. Righteousness does not consist in volition. Volition — deciding and resolving to do something — is an act of will, but necessitated by choice. It is an executive act, and is the product of a purpose or choice. It is designed as a means to an end. It is put forth to control either the attention of the intellect, the states of the sensibility, or the movements of the outward life by force. Volition is both an effect and a cause. It is the effect of a choice, purpose, intention. It is the cause of the outward life and of many of the changes both of the intellect and sensibility. Volition is a *doing*. Whatever we do we accomplish by the exercise of volition. Volition is not, in the highest sense, a free act, because it is an effect. It is itself caused. Hence, it has no moral character in itself, and moral quality can be predicated of it only as it partakes of the character of its primary cause.

3. Righteousness does not consist in proximate or subordinate choice.

I choose an ultimate, supreme end *for its own sake*. Such choice is not executive; it is not put forth to secure the end but is simply the choice of an object for its own sake. This is ultimate choice.

I purpose or choose, if possible, to secure a particular end. This is proximate or subordinate choice. Strictly speaking, this choice belongs (like volition) to the category of cause and effect. It results by necessity from the ultimate choice. In the strictest sense it is not a free act, since it is itself caused. Hence it has no moral character in itself, but, like volition, derives whatever moral quality it has from its primary cause or the ultimate choice.

4. Righteousness does not consist in any of the states or activities of the sensibility. (By the sensibility I mean that department of the mind that feels, desires, suffers, enjoys.) All the states of the sensibility are involuntary and belong to the category of cause and effect. The will cannot control them directly, nor always indirectly. This we know by consciousness. Since they are caused and not free, they can have no moral character in themselves, and, like thoughts, volitions, subordinate choices, have no moral quality except that which is derived from their primary cause.

In short: righteousness does not consist in doing anything, resolving anything, choosing anything for any secondary purpose, or in any feeling of desire, remorse, or ecstacy. None of these means can righteousness secure or produce.

II. What righteousness is.

Righteousness is moral rightness, moral recti-
tude, moral uprightness, conformity to moral law.
But what mental act or state is that which the
moral law, the law of God, requires? Law is a rule
of action. Moral law requires action — mental
action, responsible action, therefore free action.
But what particular *form* of action does moral law
require?

Free action is a certain form of action of the
will (and this is the *only* strictly free action). Christ
has taught us, by His own teaching and through
His inspired prophets and apostles, that the moral
law requires *love*, and that this is the sum of its
requirements. But what *is* this love? It cannot be
the involuntary love of the sensibility, either in the
form of emotion or affection; for these states of
mind, belonging as they do to the category of cause
and effect, cannot be the form of love demanded by
the law of God. The moral law is the law of God's
activity, the rule in conformity to which He always
acts. We are created in God's image; His rule of life
is therefore ours. The moral law requires of Him
the *same* kind of love that it does of us. (If God had
no law or rule of action, He could have no moral
character.) As our Creator and Lawgiver, He
requires of us the same love in kind and the same
perfection in degree that He Himself exercises.
"God is love." This means He loves with all the
strength of His infinite nature. He requires us to
love with all the strength of our finite nature. This

is being perfect as God is perfect.

But what is this love of God (*i.e.,* as a mental exercise)? It must be benevolence or good will, for God is a moral agent. The good of universal being is infinitely valuable in itself. God must infinitely well appreciate this. He must see and feel the moral propriety of choosing this for its own sake. He has chosen it from eternity. By His executive volitions He is endeavoring to realize it. The law which He has promulgated to govern *our* activity requires us to sympathize with His choice, His benevolence, to choose the same end that He does, for the same reason — that is, *for its own sake.*

God's infinite choice of the good of universal being is righteousness in Him, because it is the choice of the intrinsically and infinitely valuable for its own sake. It is a choice in conformity with His nature and the relations He has constituted. It must be a choice in conformity with His infinitely clear conscience or moral sense. Righteousness in God, then, is conformity to the laws of universal love or good will. It must be an ultimate, supreme, immanent, efficient preference or choice of the highest good of universal being, including His own. It must be ultimate, in that this good of being is chosen for its own sake. It must be supreme, because it is preferred to everything else. It must be immanent, because it is innate and at the very foundation of all His moral activity. It must be efficient, because, from its very nature, it must energize to secure that which is thus preferred or chosen with the whole strength of His infinite nature. This is right choice, right moral action.

The moral quality, then, of *unselfish benevolence* is righteousness or moral rightness. All subordinate choices, volitions and actions, and states of sensibility which proceed from this immanent, ultimate, supreme preference or choice, have moral character in the sense and only for the reason that they proceed from or are the natural product of unselfish benevolence. This ultimate, immanent, supreme preference is the holy heart of a moral agent. Out of it proceeds, directly or indirectly, the whole moral or spiritual life of the individual.

III. How we know what righteousness is.

I answer: By consciousness.

(a) By consciousness we know that our whole life proceeds from ultimate choice or preference. (b) By consciousness we know that conscience demands perfect, universal love or unselfish benevolence; and, by consequence, it demands all those acts and states of mind and outward courses of life that by a law of our nature proceed from unselfish benevolence. (c) By consciousness we know that conscience is satisfied with this, demands nothing more, and accepts nothing less. (d) By consciousness we know that conscience pronounces this to be right, or righteousness. (e) By consciousness we know that this is obedience to the law of God as revealed in our nature, and that when we render this obedience we are so adjusted in the will of God that we have perfect peace. We are in sympathy with God. We are at peace with God and with ourselves. Short of this we cannot be so.

This I understand to be the teaching both of our nature and the Bible. My limits will not allow me to quote Scripture to sustain this view.

IV. Lastly, how a sinner may attain to righteousness.

A sinner is a selfish moral agent. Being selfish, he will, of course, make no other than selfish efforts to become righteous. Selfishness is a state of voluntary committal to the indulgence of the sensibility. While the will is in this state of committal to self-indulgence, the soul will not and cannot put forth any righteous act. The first righteous act possible to an unregenerate sinner is to change his heart, or the supreme ultimate preference of his soul. Without this he may *outwardly* conform to the letter of God's law, but this is not righteousness. Without this he may have many exercises and states of mind which he may suppose to be Christian experience, but *these* are not righteousness. Without a change of heart he may live a perfectly outwardly moral and religious life. All this he may do for selfish reasons; but *this is not righteousness.*

I say again, his first righteous act must be to change his heart. To say that he will change this for any selfish reason is simply a contradiction, for the change of heart involves the renunciation of selfishness. How, then, can a sinner change his heart or attain to righteousness? I answer: Only by tak-

ing such a view of the character and claims of God
as to induce him to renounce his self-seeking spirit
and come into sympathy with God. To say nothing
here of possibility, the Bible reveals the fact (and
human consciousness attests the truth) that a sinner will never attain to such a view of the claims of
God as will induce him to renounce selfishness and
sympathize with God without the illumina tions of
the Holy Spirit. A sinner attains, then, to righteousness *only* through the teachings and inspirations of
the Holy Spirit.

But what is involved is this change from sin to
righteousness?

(1) It must involve confidence in God, or faith.
Without confidence a soul could not be persuaded
to change his heart, to renounce self and sympathize with God. (2) It must involve repentance. By
repentance I mean that change of mind which consists in a renunciation of self-seeking and a coming
into sympathy with God. (3) It involves a radical
change of moral attitude in respect to God and our
neighbor. All these are involved in a change of
heart. They occur simultaneously, and the presence of one implies the existence and presence of
the others.

It is by the truths of the gospel that the Holy
Spirit induces this change in sinful man. This revelation of divine love, when powerfully sent home
by the Holy Spirit, is an effectual calling. From the
above it will be seen that, while a sinner may live a
perfectly outwardly moral and religious life, a truly

regenerated soul cannot live a sinful life. The new heart does not, cannot sin. This John in his First Epistle expressly affirms. A benevolent, supreme, ultimate choice cannot produce selfish, subordinate choices or volitions.

It *is* possible for a Christian to backslide. If it were not, perseverance would be no virtue. If the change were a physical one, or a change of the very nature of the sinner, backsliding would be impossible and perseverance no virtue. It is objected to this view that backsliding must consist in going back to a selfish, ultimate preference, and, therefore, involve an adverse change of heart. What if it does? Must this not be, indeed, true? Did not Adam and Eve change their hearts from holy to sinful ones?

But may a man change his heart back and forth? I answer: Yes, or a sinner could not be required to make to himself a new heart, nor could a Christian sin after regeneration. The idea that the same person can have at the same time both a holy and a sinful heart is absurd in true philosophy, contrary to the Bible, and of most pernicious tendency. When a soul is backslidden, Christ calls upon him to repent and do his first work over again.

Righteousness is sustained in the human soul by the indwelling of Christ through faith — and in no other way. It cannot be sustained by purposes or resolutions self-originated and not inwrought by the Spirit of Christ. Through faith Christ first gains ascendancy in the human heart, and through faith He maintains this ascendancy and reigns as king in the soul.

There can be no righteousness in man back of his heart, for nothing back of this can be voluntary; therefore, there can be no righteousness in the nature of man in the sense that implies praise-worthiness or virtue.

All outward conformity to the law and commandments of God that does not proceed from Christ, working in the soul by His Holy Spirit, is *self*-righteousness. All *true* righteousness, then, is the righteousness of faith, or a righteousness secured by Christ through faith in Him.